Exploring
Ecclesiastes
& Song of
Solomon

Exploring
Ecclesiastes
& Song of
Solomon

A DEVOTIONAL COMMENTARY

GEORGE R. KNIGHT

REVIEW AND HERALD® PUBLISHING ASSOCIATION
HAGERSTOWN, MD 21740

The author assumes full responsibility for the accuracy of all facts and quotations
as cited in this book.

Unless otherwise noted, all Bible texts quoted are from the *New American Standard Bible,* copyright © 1960, 1962, 1968, 1971, 1975, 1977, 1994 by the Lockman Foundation. Used by permission.

Texts credited to Message are from *The Message.* Copyright © 1993, 1994, 1995, 1996. Used by permission of NavPress Publishing Group.

Bible texts credited to Moffatt are from: *The Bible: A New Translation,* by James Moffatt. Copyright by James Moffatt 1954. Used by permission of Harper & Row Publishers, Incorporated.

Texts credited to NEB are from *The New English Bible.* © The Delegates of the Oxford University Press and the Syndics of the Cambridge University Press 1961, 1970. Reprinted by permission.

Texts credited to NIV are from the *Holy Bible, New International Version.* Copyright © 1973, 1978, 1984, International Bible Society. Used by permission of Zondervan Bible Publishers.

Scripture quotations marked NLT are taken from the *Holy Bible,* New Living Translation, copyright © 1996. Used by permission of Tyndale House Publishers, Inc., Wheaton, Illinois 60189. All rights reserved.

Texts credited to NKJV are from the New King James Version. Copyright © 1979, 1980, 1982 by Thomas Nelson, Inc. Used by permission. All rights reserved.

Bible texts credited to NRSV are from the New Revised Standard Version of the Bible, copyright © 1989 by the Division of Christian Education of the National Council of the Churches of Christ in the U.S.A. Used by permission.

Scripture quotations marked RSV are from the *Revised Standard Version of the Bible,* copyright © 1946, 1952, 1971, by the Division of Christian Education of the National Council of the Churches of Christ in the U.S.A. Used by permission.

Texts credited to Tanakh are from *Tanakh: A New Translation of the Holy Scriptures According to the Traditional Hebrew Text.* Copyright © The Jewish Publication Society of America, Philadelphia, 1985.

Bible texts credited to TEV are from the *Good News Bible*—Old Testament: Copyright © American Bible Society 1976, 1992; New Testament: Copyright © American Bible Society 1966, 1971, 1976, 1992.

This book was
Edited by Gerald Wheeler
Cover designed by Trent Truman
Cover illustration by Trent Truman
Electronic makeup by Shirley M. Bolivar
Typeset: 11/14 Bembo

PRINTED IN U.S.A.

10 09 08 07 06   5 4 3 2 1

R&H Cataloging Service
Knight, George R.
    Exploring Ecclesiastes and Song of Solomon: a devotional commentary.

    1. Bible. O.T. Ecclesiastes and Song of Solomon—Criticism, interpretation, etc.
I. Title.

227.87

ISBN 10: 0-8280-2018-3
ISBN 13: 978-0-8280-2018-3

Dedicated to

Bonnie,
my companion
and friend,
my special
Shulammite

Contents

Book I: *Exploring Ecclesiastes*

    A Note on Wisdom Literature
    Literary Characteristics of Ecclesiastes
    The Author of Ecclesiastes
    Purpose of Ecclesiastes
    Ecclesiastes' Main Themes
    Structure of Ecclesiastes
    Outline of Ecclesiastes
    Ecclesiastes' Relevance for the Twenty-first Century
    List of Works Cited

Book II. *Exploring the Song of Solomon*

Exploring the "Exploring" Idea

E xploring *Ecclesiastes and Song of Solomon* is the fourth volume in a series of user-friendly commentaries aimed at helping people understand
the Bible better. While the books have the needs and abilities of laypeople
in mind, they will also prove beneficial to pastors and other church leaders. Beyond individual readers, the "Exploring" format will be helpful for
church study groups and in enriching participation in midweek meetings.

Each volume is best thought of as a devotional commentary. While the
treatment of each passage seeks to develop its exegetical meaning, it does
not stop there but moves on to practical application in the daily life of believers in the twenty-first century.

Rather than focusing on the details of each verse, the "Exploring" volumes seek to give readers an understanding of the themes and patterns of
each biblical book as a whole and how each passage fits into its context. As
a result, they do not attempt to solve all of the problems or answer all the
questions related to a given portion of Scripture.

In an effort to be user-friendly these devotional commentaries on the
Old and New Testaments present the entire text of each biblical book
treated The volumes divide the text into "bite-sized" portions that are included immediately before the comments on the passage. Thus readers do
not have to flip back and forth between their Bibles and the commentary.

The commentary sections aim at being long enough to significantly
treat a topic, but short enough for individual, family, or group readings.

Exploring Ecclesiastes and Song of Solomon is the first Old Testament
volume in the series. Unlike the New Testament volumes, which fea-

ture my own translation from the original Greek, I have chosen to use the updated edition of the *New American Standard Bible* for this particular volume.

George R. Knight
Andrews University
Berrien Springs, Michigan

Foreword

I have found Ecclesiastes and Song of Solomon to be two of the more challenging books of the Bible. But then I have also discovered life itself is daunting. Both books reflect not theory, but life as it is experienced, with Ecclesiastes focusing on the life of the mind and the Song centering on the romantic.

Of the two, Ecclesiastes relates more naturally to my way of thinking. My doctoral degree is in philosophy; and my graduate study in theology, philosophy, history, sociology, and psychology, as well as my teaching and writing, has taken place in the context of a search for the meaning of life—a quest that I continue as I enter retirement.

I have struggled with Ecclesiastes through the years, but have wrestled even more with the Song of Solomon. In my earlier days it was a book that I tended to skip over or read through quickly. But in the past couple years I have come to see it as a scriptural jewel that I had vastly undervalued. I now know that I will be a better husband because of my study of that little book. I should note that my remarks on it tend to be more impressionistic than technical. Its author paints pictures that need to be imagined rather than providing us with architectural drawings that spell out every thought in exactitude.

This devotional commentary can be read as a freestanding book or it can be utilized with the on line study guide developed to accompany it. The study guide to *Exploring Ecclesiastes and Song of Solomon* will provide those who employ it with an opportunity to let the biblical books speak to them personally through structured questions before they turn to the commentary itself. (To download and print the free study guide, go to www.AdventistBookCenter.com, find the book *Exploring Ecclesiastes and Song of Solomon*, then "click for details" and follow the instructions near the bottom of the page for downloading the study guide.)

I would like to express special appreciation to my wife. This has been her first book-length attempt to render what I like to think of as handwriting into computerized format. And as always I want to thank Gerald Wheeler, who has supplied me with editorial expertise for more than 20 years; Jeannette Johnson, who always encourages me in my writing; and to the administration of Andrews University, who have provided me with support and time for research and writing for three decades.

Exploring
Ecclesiastes

Introduction to Ecclesiastes

What are we to do with a book that doubts the meaning of life, points out the futility and uselessness of work, treats death as the final end, and admonishes its readers to eat, drink, and be merry since this present life is all we have? Does it even belong in the Bible? One commentator calls it "the strangest book in the Bible" (Scott, p. 191), while the ancient rabbis debated as to whether reading it imparted ritual "uncleanness to hands" because it was inspired and therefore holy, or whether it was just another human production (*Mishnah,* Yadayim 3:5).

Through the centuries the biblical book we call Ecclesiastes has made many religious people uncomfortable both because of what it plainly states and what it fails to say. Phyllis Trible notes that it has a "haunting tone and tantalizing power to evoke diverse interpretations" (see Trible, p. 231). Yet with all of its problems it is still in the Bible. Why? That is the question we will address in this introduction to a unique volume in the biblical library.

A Note on Wisdom Literature

Not only does Ecclesiastes focus on strange topics, but it avoids those at the very center of most biblical books. Where, for example, do we find any mention of Abraham, Isaac, and Jacob? Why do we not hear of the land of Canaan?

Those are important questions. In answering them we need to realize that Ecclesiastes belongs to a type of writing that has come to be known as wisdom literature. "The most striking characteristic" of wisdom literature, Roland Murphy points out, "is the absence of what one normally considers as typically Israelite or Jewish. There is no mention of the promises to the patriarchs, the Exodus and Moses, the covenant and Sinai, the promise to David (2 Sam 7), and so forth. . . . Wisdom does not re-present the actions of God in Israel's history; it deals with daily human experience" (Murphy, *Tree of Life*, p. 1).

Wisdom literature centers around such topics as instruction for successful living and the discussion of perplexing topics involving the meaning and significance of human existence. Near Eastern wisdom literature comes in two major types: (1) proverbial wisdom made up of "short, pithy sayings which state rules for personal happiness and welfare or condense the wisdom of experience and make acute observations about life" and (2) "contemplative or speculative wisdom—monologues, dialogues, or essays which delve into basic problems of human existence such as the meaning of life and the problem of suffering" (La Sor, pp. 533, 534). The biblical book of Proverbs is a good example of the first type of wisdom and Job of the second. Ecclesiastes contains both types, with contemplative/speculative wisdom predominating in the first half and proverbial wisdom emerging into larger play in the second.

Beyond those three books, certain of the psalms along with Song of Solomon and Lamentations share an affinity with wisdom style and content. We should note that wisdom literature is not restricted to the Bible. It appears in the apocryphal books of Ecclesiasticus (also known as the Wisdom of Sirach) and the Wisdom of Solomon and in the literatures of Egypt, Mesopotamia, and other Near Eastern cultures. Interestingly, we notice a great deal of overlap between the wisdom contained in the Bible and that of the surrounding cultures. The reason for that commonality is that wisdom literature focuses on the human situation, and people face the same sorts of intellectual and practical questions and problems from one culture to the next. Thus both Israel and its neighbors faced questions dealing with the meaning of life and death or the profit of expending energy in useful work rather than merely laying around all day. As a result, proverbs found in one society often appeared in the others as well. Many observations based on study and reflection tended to be universal among the wisdom writers of the ancient world.

That does not mean, however, that Israel's wisdom literature was secular or that it did not differ from the wisdom of its neighbors. "Far from it! No one can read Job, Proverbs, or Ecclesiastes without hearing overtones of Israel's distinctive faith. For the true Israelite all wisdom stemmed from God and was available to human beings only because they were creatures of God, capable of receiving his revelation. But more than this," from the perspective of Israelite wisdom, "only the devout worshipper, who feared God, could really begin to be wise." Wisdom was a gift of God, "part of his order in creation" (La Sor, p. 545).

Literary Characteristics of Ecclesiastes

The book of Ecclesiastes is as close as we come to a strictly philosophical approach to life and truth in the Bible. For most of the book the author does not base his conclusions on revelation but on observation and experience and reflections on them both. The core of his literary style is first-person narratives in which the author relates his observations about the absurdity of life. As the book progresses the writer enriches the narrative with proverbs ("He who loves money will not be satisfied with money," 5:10), rhetorical questions ("What gain has the worker from his toil?" 3:9, RSV), and metaphors and allegory (comparing death to a "silver cord" breaking and a pitcher shattering, 12:6).

Ecclesiastes is not the easiest biblical book to read. Like Job, O. S. Rankin notes, Ecclesiastes "has the distinction of investigating a problem which besets mankind in general and for which there is no easy solution—indeed no solution offered by human resources" (Rankin, p. 19). You will probably note that as the author struggles with life's great issues he does not appear to be altogether consistent. That disturbs some readers, but it doesn't bother the author of Ecclesiastes. His answer to the charge of being inconsistent would undoubtedly be, "So what?—life itself is full of inconsistencies."

The book of Ecclesiastes is not for casual reading. As Michael Fox puts it, "understanding Ecclesiastes requires engagement, exploration, dissent, and rethinking—the very activities that characterize" the writer himself (Fox, *Ecclesiastes*, p. xxii). While the book does not lend itself to easy reading, a reflective study of it is highly rewarding. God put this book in the Bible for those who choose to grapple with the mighty issues of life and meaning.

At this point you may want to turn to Ecclesiastes itself and scan it. As you go through the book, look for overall patterns and meaning rather than line by line understanding. Your reading will be enriched if you keep such key passages as 1:2; 12:8; and 12:13,14 in mind. Those texts, as we note later, are central in grasping the overall significance of the book's message.

The Author of Ecclesiastes

While Israel's approach to wisdom had undoubtedly began earlier than the time of Solomon, it definitely took on a more vigorous life during his reign. The Bible tells us that "God gave Solomon wisdom and understanding beyond measure, and largeness of mind like the sand on the seashore, so that Solomon's wisdom surpassed the wisdom of all the people of the east, and all the wisdom of Egypt. For he was wiser than all other men, wiser than Ethan the Ezrahite, and Heman, Calcol, and Darda, the son of Mahol; and his fame was in all the nations round about. He also uttered three thousand proverbs; and his songs were a thousand and five. He spoke of trees, from the cedar that is in Lebanon to the hyssop that grows out of the wall; he spoke also of beasts, and of birds, and of reptiles, and of fish. And men came from all peoples to hear the wisdom of Solomon, and from all the kings of the earth, who had heard of his wisdom" (1 Kings 4:29-34, RSV).

Given the reputation of Solomon and the wealth and power of his court, it is no accident that Israelite wisdom literature, both biblical and nonbiblical, became predominantly attached to his name. Historically people have viewed Solomon as the author of Ecclesiastes, even though the book itself makes no such claim. In fact, it doesn't even mention the name of Solomon. On the other hand it does imply that the author was the "son of David, king in Jerusalem" (1:1) and that he himself had been "king over Israel in Jerusalem" (verse 12). The first chapter also has the author saying, "Behold I have magnified and increased wisdom more than all who were over Jerusalem before me; and my mind has observed a wealth of wisdom and knowledge" (verse 16).

Those who hold to Solomonic authorship generally believe that he "wrote Ecclesiastes in his old age . . . , and indeed [the author] gives the impression of speaking from the vantage point of an old man looking back on life" (Fox, *Ecclesiastes*, p. x). From this perspective, some see Solomon looking back over his wasted years and pointing to a better way (White, *Prophets and Kings*, pp. 79, 85).

Others claim that the author was not Solomon but that he used "Solomon's experiences as the backdrop for his argument. How better could a wise man illustrate the limits of wisdom, pleasure, prestige, wealth, and achievement than to cite Solomon's experiences? In a later setting," the argument runs, "the younger wise man donned Solomon's robes to explore the deficiencies of a way of life based on Solomonic values" (Hubbard, *Beyond Futility*, p. 8).

Ecclesiastes itself calls the author Qoheleth (also spelled Koheleth and Qohelet) or *the* Qoheleth (12:8). The word often gets translated as "The Preacher" in English. From the very first verse we read that we are going to hear "the words of the Preacher."

We should note that nothing in Ecclesiastes itself conclusively demonstrates that Solomon is not the author. Nor is there anything that proves that he must be. The good news is that the message of the book does not depend upon our knowledge of the writer's proper name. It seems best to follow the lead of the inspired book and call him the Preacher. (For issues dealing with the possibility of Ecclesiastes having more than one author/editor, see the comments in section 20).

Purpose of Ecclesiastes

"Anyone to whom the book of Ecclesiastes is not a puzzle," claims David Hubbard, "has not yet read it" (Hubbard, *Beyond Futility*, p. 7). Perhaps the most basic purpose of the book is to get people to think. Certainly readers will find themselves wondering why the faith and the certainties so nicely expressed in many other parts of the Old Testament are seemingly missing from Ecclesiastes. For example, whereas the psalmist looks upon the creation around him and reflects about what God has done for His people, the Preacher examines the same world and finds it an unending round of meaninglessness. Whereas the prophets call for reforming an unjust society, "this man looks out on the same kind of society, shrugs his shoulders and says, 'It's the system, you can't beat it' (*eg* Eccles. 5:8)" (Davidson, p. 5).

If thinking lies at the heart of the Preacher's book, thoughts about the meaningfulness of life is the blood that flows through that heart. To have meaning, events must be able to be interpreted in terms of a comprehensible picture. In a sensible world, "the righteous *should* be rewarded, the wicked punished; the one who toils *should* get to enjoy the full fruits of his work; the wise *should* have a life the polar opposite of the fool's, and something *should* distinguish them in death. A life with a strict correspondence between deed and consequence, virtue and reward, vice and punishment, would make sense." But the Preacher does not see that kind of a world. Contradiction seems to weigh life down in the everyday world and meaning appears to have collapsed (Fox, *Ecclesiastes,* p. xxx). At the focal point of the book we encounter a frustrated person wrestling with the point of existence. A fundamental purpose of his book is to get his readers to grapple with him.

That struggle for meaning is on the surface of the book. More subtle is the book's function as a pointer toward God as the only hope for purpose in a messed up world. He has vividly described the senselessness of a despairing world "under curse and apart from God." But beyond senselessness and despair, "in a masterfully succinct manner . . . the book ends with three phrases that point away from skeptical thinking and toward a theology consonant with the rest of the OT" (Longman, pp. 40, 39):

1. "Fear God,"
2. "Keep His commandments," and
3. "God will bring every act to judgment" (Eccl. 12:13, 14).

Thus the ultimate goal of Ecclesiastes is to point beyond a life of pessimism without God to a just and righteous deity who will eventually right all wrongs.

Ecclesiastes' Major Themes

Two main themes—the absurdity of life and the limitations of unaided human knowledge—run throughout the book of Ecclesiastes and hover near the center of each of its discussions. Beyond those dominating themes lurk ongoing subthemes related to death, joy, and the implications of the early chapters of Genesis. The book climaxes with the idea that life without God has no meaning, a claim that is the opposite side of the coin from the book's two dominating themes and one tied directly to the subthemes.

1. *The absurdity of life and its activities.* One of the Preacher's key words is *hebel,* which at its most basic level means "vapor." Vapor, of course, lacks substance. Most Bible scholars generally translate the word into English as "vanity," but in most cases we might better render it as "absurd" or "senseless." *Hebel* occurs 64 times in the Bible, 30 of them in the 12 short chapters of Ecclesiastes.

The Preacher framed his book with multiple uses of *hebel*. "'Vanity of vanities,' says the Preacher" in the book's second verse, "'vanity of vanities! All is vanity.'" In like manner we read near the end of the book: "'Vanity of vanities,' says the Preacher, 'all is vanity'" (12:8). We should note that Hebrew does not have a superlative form as we do in English when, for example, we say that "she is the brightest student" or that "that is the best book." Rather, Hebrew repeats the word to indicate that something is the best. The title Song of Songs, for example, means that it is the best of all songs. And it is clear from the Preacher's repeated use of *hebel* that he is talking about something that is the most absurd or meaningless. And what is *hebel* or absurd? Life's activities and our ultimate death! The Preacher will have a great deal to say about those topics. His discussion fills the chapters of his book. In short, all of life and its activities "under the sun" are absurd or meaningless. Even death is meaningless, since, from the perspective of this world, good and bad people all end up in the same situation (2:14-16; 9:1-6; 3:16-22), and it could be that some unworthy person will inherit the wealth that a good person worked so hard to amass (2:18, 19). That life and its activities are meaningless is the repeated refrain of the Preacher. But he contexts that refrain by the phrase "under the sun."

2. *Human wisdom is limited and is inadequate for unlocking the meaning of existence.* The Preacher repeatedly refers to human wisdom as being "under the sun," which Ecclesiastes 1:13, 14 equates with "under heaven." In typical Near Eastern fashion the Preacher divides reality into two realms: one being the abode of humans—"under the sun"—and the other being the dwelling place of God in the heavens, or what we might call "above the sun."

"Under the sun" and "under heaven" appear more than 30 times in Ecclesiastes with "under the sun" the phrase used most often. The author employs the two phrases to indicate something on earth or from an earthly perspective. Thus when the Preacher questions the advantage of work done "under the sun" he means earthly accomplishments. The bulk of Ecclesiastes is an "under the sun" evaluation of life. It represents an earthly, human perspective rather than a heavenly viewpoint.

Basic to the logic of Ecclesiastes is that "God is in heaven and you are on the earth" (5:2). We don't see as He does. We evaluate the meaning of life from the perspective of what we observe, hear, and experience. But

God witnesses the full picture from what might be thought of as an "above the sun" perspective. Undergirding the Preacher's observations is the idea that from a purely earthly viewpoint all is meaningless, vain, absurd, *hebel*. But also underlying them is the divine perspective that shows up occasionally throughout the book and is most pronounced in the final verses. That divine viewpoint holds the key to true meaning.

In short, human wisdom is limited. It is inadequate to explain the meaning of existence. "The Preacher's point," Michael Eaton observes, "is that what is to be seen with sheer pessimism 'under the sun' may be seen differently in the light of faith in the generosity of God" (Eaton, p. 45). From another point of view, James Crenshaw points out that "Qoheleth wished to penetrate to the underlying meaning of all knowledge," but that from his "under the sun" perspective "he lacked the key that would unlock the vault within which ultimate purpose lay untouched" (Crenshaw, *Old Testament Wisdom,* p. 121).

3. *The injustice of death.* The Preacher, perhaps more than any other biblical author, is obsessed with the problem of death. For him death is what might be thought of as the ultimate absurdity, especially since from his "under the sun" viewpoint there appears to exist no hope beyond the grave. The ultimate injustice is that "the wise man dies just like the fool" (2:14-16, RSV). The good and the evil share the same fate in the grave (9:2). And when it comes to death, notes the Preacher, humans are no better off than animals. "Man has no advantage over the beasts. . . . All go to one place; all are from the dust, and all turn to dust again" (3:19, 20, RSV). Death is the end. The dead "know nothing, . . . they have no more reward," and even "the memory of them is lost" (9:5, RSV). To the Preacher as he views life from the perspective of "under the sun" the grave is the end. His thoughts bothered him so much that at one point he concludes that those who were dead already were more fortunate than those who were still alive and thus had to struggle with meaning in an absurd existence (4:2).

4. *The need to enjoy life while people still have it.* The rather contradictory Preacher in the long run is quite sure that life is better than death, exclaiming at one point that a live dog is better than a dead lion (9:4). Repeatedly he urges his readers to enjoy life (see, e.g., 2:24; 3:12, 22; 5:18; 8:15; 9:7-9; 11:7-10). One scholar has even described the author as a

"preacher of joy" (see Whybray, p. xxii). But such a conclusion misses the subtleties of the argument. After all, what Ecclesiastes tells us about the life of enjoyment has a specific context. "I command enjoyment," the Preacher declares, "for man has no good thing *under the sun* but to eat, and drink, and enjoy himself, for this will go with him in his toil through the days of life which God gives him *under the sun*" (8:15, RSV; cf. 5:18, italics supplied). Murphy points out that what appears to be an enthusiastic endorsement of the life of joy is really nothing better than a "concession to circumstances" rather than "unqualified approval" (Murphy, *Tree of Life,* p. 54). In other words, a bit of enjoyment is about all of value you can get in your race with death in an absurd existence. But in the long run the Preacher is fully aware that earthly pleasures are fleeting, meaningless. He had tried worldly pleasure and found it absurd (2:1-11). But if you live in an "under the sun" world that is about as good as you can do.

5. *The Preacher presses home the implications of the early chapters of Genesis.* The biblical picture of the post-fall human condition in Genesis surfaces throughout Ecclesiastes. Genesis 2:7, for example, finds God creating humans out of the dust of the earth and breathing into them the breath of life. Ecclesiastes pictures death as the reverse of creation, with the dust returning to the earth and the breath (often translated as "spirit") going back to God who gave it (12:7 cf. Gen. 3:19). More important is the fact that Genesis 2 and 3 set the stage for Ecclesiastes' "under the sun" perspective by showing how the entrance of sin led to a life of frustrating toil (Gen. 3:17, 18) and death (3:19). The separation of humanity from God (3:8-10, 22-24) created the meaninglessness of the "under the sun" life expounded upon by the Preacher. As Duane Garrett points out, "the presentation of God in Ecclesiastes as absent and hidden arises directly from Gen 3 (where humanity loses access to God)." Others have observed that the Preacher's oft repeated refrain of *hebel* ("meaninglessness") may be a play on the Hebrew name of Abel, the murdered son of Adam (Garrett, pp. 278, 279).

6. *The only answer to the meaning of life is to fear God and to live according to His principles.* Throughout the body of Ecclesiastes the author has demonstrated that earthly ("under the sun") activities are meaningless *(hebel)* and that the best one can do is to enjoy to the fullness of one's abilities the fleeting pleasures of life as a person slides toward the dark and silent grave.

If one is looking for answers to the meaning of life, the Preacher has proved that we will not find any satisfactory ones from a strictly human "under the sun" perspective. The meaning of life, he notes in his conclusion to the book, is discovered in the "above the sun" realm. If earthly strivings and human reasonings all end in meaninglessness, then people must look to God, fear Him, and do His will (12:13). In other words, the only solution is to reverse the effects of the Genesis Fall. Ecclesiastes concludes with the thought that in the end God will set all things right (12:14). Only then will the world make sense.

Structure of Ecclesiastes

Trying to figure out the structure of Ecclesiastes has puzzled Bible students for generations. One scholar notes that the book "resists organization" (see Trible, p. 232), another suggests that it has virtually no organization (Delitzsch, pp. 185-188), and a third concludes that "the structure of Ecclesiastes is . . . not a hierarchical outline but a kind of wandering among several topics" (Garrett, p. 270). Roland Murphy sums up the problem by stating that "there is simply no agreement concerning the structure of Ecclesiastes. . . . It seems to lack any order from the point of view of logical progression of thought, but of course that depends upon whose 'logic' is at issue" (Murphy, *Wisdom Literature,* p. 127).

Picking up on that point, David Hubbard and his colleagues argue for Hebrew logic, noting that the Preacher's approach rests upon (1) "the typically Semitic repetitive nature of his arguments to demonstrate his theme," and (2) "the use of clusters of proverbs, 'words of advice' to clarify or reinforce the argument" (La Sor, p. 590).

While Ecclesiastes' structure may not fit the norms of modern Western argument, that does not mean that it lacks structured markers altogether. Two stand out in the text as being especially important. First are the bracket texts located at Ecclesiastes 1:2 and 12:8. Both read the same: "'Vanity of vanities,' says the Preacher, 'all is vanity.'" That repeated phrase encapsulates the major arguments in a manner that indicates that it is a major theme of the book. The second structured marker is related to the first in that the bracket texts separate the main body of the book from its prologue and epilogue in such a way that we might think of the book as "framed wisdom autobiography" (see Longman, p. 17).

Outline of Ecclesiastes

I. Introduction (1:1-3)
    A. Title (1:1)
    B. BRACKET TEXT—all is complete vanity (1:2)
    C. Theme activated (1:3)

II. Theme demonstrated—round no. 1 (1:4-2:26)
    A. Meaninglessness of the cycle of life (1:4-11)
    B. Meaninglessness of human wisdom (1:12-18)
    C. Meaninglessness of pleasure and wealth (2:1-11)
    D. Meaninglessness in the face of death (2:12-17)
    E. Meaninglessness of toil (2:18-23)
    F. *Alternate conclusion:* Enjoy life now as God gives it (2:24-26)

III. Theme demonstrated—round no. 2 (3:1-4:16)
    A. Uselessness of striving against the round of nature (3:1-11,14, 15)
    B. *Alternate conclusion:* Enjoy life now as God gives it (3:12, 13)
    C. Uselessness of striving against oncoming death (3:16-21)
    D. *Alternate conclusion:* Enjoy life now as God gives it (3:22)
    E. Uselessness of striving against oppression (4:1-3)
    F. Uselessness of striving for wealth by toil (4:4-8)
    G. Words of advice—importance of the support of another person (4:9-12)
    H. Uselessness of striving to retain popularity (4:13-16)

IV. Words of advice (5:1-12)
    A. Honor God in worship (5:1-3)
    B. Pay your vows (5:4-7)
    C. Do not expect justice in government (5:8, 9)
    D. Do not overvalue wealth (5:10-12)

V. Theme demonstrated—round no. 3 (5:13-6:12)
    A. The frustration of bad investments (5:13-17)
    B. *Alternate conclusion:* Enjoy life now as God gives it (5:18-20)
    C. The frustration of wealth that cannot be enjoyed (6:1-9)
    D. The frustration of fate (6:10-12)

VI. Words of Advice (7:1-8:9)
    A. Honor is better than luxury (7:1)
    B. Sobriety is better than levity (7:2-7)
    C. Patience is better than haste (7:8-10)

D. Wisdom with wealth is better than wisdom alone (7:11, 12)

E. Resignation is better than indignation (7:13, 14)

F. Moderation is better than intemperance (7:15-22)

G. The shortcomings of wisdom (7:23-25)

H. More men have wisdom than women, but no one is righteous (7:26-29)

I. Advice on government service (8:1-6)

J. Limitations on human authority (8:7-9)

VII. Theme demonstrated—round no. 4 (8:10-9:12)

A. Justice is uncertain (8:10-14)

B. *Alternate conclusion:* Enjoy life now as God gives it (8:15)

C. God's ways are unknowable (8:16, 17)

D. Death is a certainty (9:1-6)

E. *Alternate conclusion:* Enjoy life now as God gives it (9:7-10)

F. Life is uncertain (9:11, 12)

VIII. Words of advice (9:13-12:7)

A. Wisdom is better than might (9:13-16)

B. Wisdom is better than folly (9:17-10:15)

C. Important maxims (10:16-20)

D. Business maxims (11:1-8)

E. Enjoy life before death comes (11:9-12:7)

IX. Conclusion (12:8-14)

A. BRACKET TEXT—all is complete vanity (12:8)

B. The goal of the Preacher (12:9, 10)

C. The function of the Preacher (12:11, 12)

D. The duty of humans and the justice of God (12:13, 14)

Ecclesiastes' Relevance for the Twenty-first Century

Ecclesiastes is an exciting book because it deals directly with life, with the challenges and questions provided by daily experience. Who of us hasn't felt the sting of injustice or the indignity of death and cried out "Why?" Beyond that, who has not mumbled something less than flattering about God in the face of life's perplexities and injustices?

The Preacher meets us where we are in daily life. James Crenshaw bares his soul when he writes that "for many years I have been fascinated with Qohlet, perhaps because he makes my own skepticism appear solidly biblical. Like him, I observe discrepancy between the vision of a just world, which I refuse to relinquish, and reality as I perceive it." That difference, he notes, provides an urgency to our theological probings (Crenshaw, *Ecclesiastes,* p. 53).

One question drives the Preacher: "Where can I find meaning?" Such a quest is just as pressing today as it was in his time. That is particularly so for those people like the Preacher who no longer find themselves satisfied by the simplistic answers taught them in their youth.

Ecclesiastes provides a twofold basis for unlocking the mysteries of life and death. On one level the Preacher sets forth the absolute fruitlessness of seeking to find ultimate meaning by human reason alone. "Under the sun" knowledge merely leads to frustration. In fact, the more people know the more frustrated they become. But pointing beyond that fruitlessness, the Preacher directs us to an "above the sun" approach to meaning in his last verses when he tells us that the answer is to fear God. He echoes Psalm 111:10, which tells us that fearing God is the beginning of wisdom. The most relevant message of Ecclesiastes is that humans can't get by on their own. They need God and His wisdom to make sense out of the hard questions of life and death. The message of the Preacher prepares people for the coming of the gospel even though it does so at a subliminal level. But ultimately the great issues of life and death find resolution in the crucifixion and resurrection of Christ who comes to hold the keys of death and the grave (Rev. 1:18).

Another point of relevance is that Ecclesiastes provides each of us with an integrating point for our daily lives. Meaningful living in the twenty-first century takes place in the fear of God and in the doing of His will in our lives day by day (Eccl. 12:13).

Finally, for those of us troubled with life's injustices we have the promise that God will bring everything—both the good and the evil—into judgment. Justice, the Preacher assures us, will have its day. That promise has ultimate relevance for each of us.

The very themes reflected in the closing verses of Ecclesiastes surface again in what the Bible pictures as the last messages to go to the world before the Second Advent. The theme of the Preacher's concluding remarks will be proclaimed again by the angels at the end of time who declare that the hour of God's judgment has come and that God's people will keep His commandments (cf. Eccl. 12:13, 14; Rev. 14:6, 7, 12). Thus Ecclesiastes will have eschatological and missiological relevance to the end of time.

List of Works Cited

Atkins, Gaius Glenn. "The Book of Ecclesiastes: Exposition." In *The Interpreter's Bible*, George Arthur Buttrick, ed. Nashville: Abingdon, 1956, vol. 5, pp. 1–88.

Barton, George Aaron. *A Critical and Exegetical Commentary on the Book of Ecclesiastes*. The International Critical Commentary. Edinburgh: T. & T. Clarke, 1908.

Bettmann, Otto L. *The Good Old Days—They Were Terrible!* New York: Random House, 1974.

Bonhoeffer, Dietrich. *Letters and Papers From Prison,* enl. ed. Eberhard Bethge, trans. New York: Macmillan, 1972.

Botterweck, G. Johannes, Helmer Ringgren, and Heinz-Josef Fabry, eds. *Theological Dictionary of the Old Testament*, vol. 13, David E. Green, trans. Grand Rapids: Eerdmans, 2004.

Brown, William P. *Ecclesiastes*. Interpretation: A Bible Commentary for Teaching and Preaching. Louisville: John Knox, 2000.

Camus, Albert. *The Myth of Sisyphus, and Other Essays*. Justin O'Brien, trans. New York: Vintage, 1955.

———. *The Stranger*. Stuart Gilbert, trans. New York: Vintage, 1954.

Crenshaw, James L. *Ecclesiastes*. Old Testament Library. Philadelphia: Westminster, 1987.

———. *Education in Ancient Israel: Across the Deadening Silence*. New York: Doubleday, 1998.

———. *Old Testament Wisdom: An Introduction,* rev. and enl. Louisville: Westminster John Knox, 1998.

Davidson, Robert. *Ecclesiastes and the Song of Solomon*. The Daily Study Bible. Louisville: Westminster John Knox, 1986.

Davis, Ellen F. *Proverbs, Ecclesiastes, and the Song of Songs*. Westminster Bible Companion. Louisville: Westminster John Knox, 2000.

Delitzsch, Franz. *Commentary on the Song of Songs and Ecclesiastes*. M. G. Easton, trans. Grand Rapids: Eerdmans, n.d.

Dorsey, David A. *The Literary Structure of the Old Testament: A Commentary on Genesis-Malachi*. Grand Rapids: Baker, 1999.

Eaton, Michael A. *Ecclesiastes*. Tyndale Old Testament Commentaries. Downers Grove, Ill.: Inter-Varsity, 1983.

Ehlke, Roland Cap. *Ecclesiastes, Song of Songs*. St. Louis: Concordia, 1994.

Farmer, Kathleen A. *Who Knows What Is Good? A Commentary on the Books of Proverbs and Ecclesiastes*. International Theological Commentary. Grand Rapids: Eerdmans, 1991.

Fox, Michael V. *Ecclesiastes*. The JPS Bible Commentary. Philadelphia: Jewish Publication Society, 2004.

————. *A Time to Tear Down and A Time to Build Up: A Rereading of Ecclesiastes*. Grand Rapids: Eerdmans, 1999.

Garrett, Duane A. *Proverbs, Ecclesiastes, Song of Songs*. The New American Commentary. Nashville: Broadman, 1993.

Gray, John. *Men Are From Mars, Women Are From Venus,* New York: HarperCollins, 1992.

Harris, R. Laird, Gleason L. Archer, Jr., and Bruce K. Waltke, eds. *Theological Wordbook of the Old Testament,* 2 vols. Chicago: Moody, 1980.

Hendricks, Rhoda A., trans. and ed. *Classical Gods and Heros: Myths as Told by Ancient Authors*. New York: Morrow Quill, 1974.

Hendry, George S. "Ecclesiastes." In *The New Bible Commentary,* rev. ed. D. Guthrie and J. A. Motyer, eds. Grand Rapids: Eerdmans, 1970, pp. 570-578.

Hengstenberg, Ernest W. *A Commentary on Ecclesiastes*. n. p.: Sovereign Grace Publishers, 1960.

Hobbes, Thomas. *Leviathan*. A Norton Critical Edition, Richard E. Flathman and David Johnston, eds. New York: W. W. Norton, 1997.

Hubbard, David Allen. *Beyond Futility: Messages of Hope From the Book of Ecclesiastes*. Grand Rapids: Eerdmans, 1976.

————. *Ecclesiastes, Song of Solomon*. The Communicator's Commentary. Dallas: Word, 1991.

Jastrow, Morris, Jr. *A Gentle Cynic*. Philadelphia: J. P. Lippincott, 1919.

Kaiser, Walter C., Jr. *Ecclesiastes: Total Life*. Everyman's Bible Commentary. Chicago: Moody, 1979.

Kidner, Derek, *The Message of Ecclesiastes*. The Bible Speaks Today. Downers Grove, Ill.: Inter-Varsity, 1976.

————. *The Wisdom of Proverbs, Job & Ecclesiastes: An Introduction to Wisdom Literature*. Downers Grove, Ill.: InterVarsity, 1985.

Krüger, Thomas. *Qoheleth*, O. C. Dean Jr., trans. Hermeneia—A Critical and Historical Commentary on the Bible. Minneapolis: Fortress, 2004.

La Sor, William Sanford, David Allen Hubbard, and Frederic Wm. Bush, *Old Testament Survey: The Message, Form, and Background of the Old Testament*. Grand Rapids: Eerdmans, 1982.

Leupold, H. C. *Exposition of Ecclesiastes*. Grand Rapids: Baker, 1966.

Loader, J. A. *Ecclesiastes: A Practical Commentary*. John Vriend, trans. Grand Rapids: Eerdmans, 1986.

Lohfink, Norbert. *Qoheleth*, Sean McEvenue, trans. Continental Commentaries. Minneapolis: Fortress, 2003.

Longman, Tremper, III. *The Book of Ecclesiastes*. The New International Commentary on the Old Testament. Grand Rapids: Eerdmans, 1998.

MacLaren, Alexander. *Esther, Job, Proverbs, and Ecclesiastes*. Exposition of Holy Scripture. Grand Rapids: Eerdmans, 1938.

Mishnah: A New Translation. Jacob Neusner, trans. New Haven, Conn.: Yale, 1988.

Morris, Desmond. *The Naked Ape*. New York: Dell, 1969.

Murphy, Roland E. *Ecclesiastes*. Word Biblical Commentary. Nashville: Thomas Nelson, 1992.

————. *The Tree of Life: An Exploration of Biblical Wisdom Literature*. New York: Doubleday, 1990.

————. *Wisdom Literature: Job, Proverbs, Ruth, Canticles, Ecclesiastes, and Esther*. The Forms of the Old Testament Literature, vol. 13. Grand Rapids: Eerdmans, 1981.

Murphy, Roland E. and Elizabeth Huwiler. *Proverbs, Ecclesiastes, Song of Songs*. New International Biblical Commentary. Peabody, Mass.: Hendrickson, 1999.

Nichol, Francis D., ed. "Ecclesiastes." In *The Seventh-day Adventist Bible Commentary*, 7 vols. Washington, D.C.: Review and Herald, 1953-1957, vol. 3, pp. 1055-1105.

Postman, Neil. *Amusing Ourselves to Death: Public Discourse in the Age of Show Business*, new edition. New York: Penguin, 2005.

Pritchard, James B., ed. *Ancient Near Eastern Texts Relating to the Old Testament*, 3d ed. with supplement. Princeton, N. J.: Princeton, 1969.

Provan, Iain. *Ecclesiastes, Song of Songs*. The NIV Application Commentary. Grand Rapids: Zondervan, 2001.

Rankin, O. S. "The Book of Ecclesiastes: Introduction and Exegesis." In *The Interpreter's Bible*, George Arthur Buttrick, ed. Nashville: Abingdon, 1956, vol. 5, pp. 1-88.

Scott, R. B. Y. *Proverbs, Ecclesiastes*. The Anchor Bible. New York: Doubleday, 1965.

Seow, C. L. *Ecclesiastes*. The Anchor Bible. New York: Doubleday, 1997.

Towner, W. Sibley. "The Book of Ecclesiastes." In *The New Interpreter's Bible*. Leander E. Keck, ed. Nashville: Abingdon, 1997, vol. 5, pp. 265-360.

Trible, Phyllis. "Ecclesiastes." In *The Books of the Bible*, Bernhard W. Anderson, ed. New York: Charles Scribner's Sons, 1989, vol. 1, pp. 231-239.

VanGemeren, Willem A., ed. *New International Dictionary of Old Testament Theology & Exegesis*, 5 vols. Grand Rapids: Zondervan, 1997.

White, Ellen G. *Education*. Mountain View, Calif.: Pacific Press, 1952.

————. *The Story of Prophets and Kings: As Illustrated in the Captivity and Restoration of Israel*. Mountain View, Calif.: Pacific Press, 1943.

Whybray, R. N. *Ecclesiastes*. The New Century Bible Commentary. Grand Rapids: Eerdmans, 1989.

Wright, J. Robert, ed. *Proverbs, Ecclesiastes, Song of Solomon*. Ancient Christian Commentary on Scripture. Downers Grove, Ill.: InterVarsity, 2005.

Wright, J. Stafford. "Ecclesiastes." In *The Expositor's Bible Commentary*, Frank E. Gaebelein, ed. Grand Rapids: Zondervan, 1991, vol. 5, pp. 1135-1197.

Part I

Meaninglessness Introduced

Ecclesiastes 1:1-3

1. Setting the Stage

Ecclesiastes 1:1-3

[1] The words of the Preacher, the son of David, king in Jerusalem.
[2] "Vanity of vanities," says the Preacher,
"Vanity of vanities! All is vanity."
[3] What advantage does man have in all his work
Which he does under the sun?

What kind of a preacher would begin his message by telling his readers that everything is meaningless and that working has no advantages? Verse 1 calls the author of Ecclesiastes "the Preacher," but one writer quips that it is an interesting title since "few congregations would put up with this preacher for very long" (Davidson, p. 6). Some have suggested that perhaps "the Philosopher" or "the Professor" might be a better translation, given his approach to his subject matter.

But "the Preacher" has generally won out as the preferred translation since *koheleth* (also spelled *qoheleth* and *qohelet*) means something like "one who does something in the assembly *(kahal),*" (Fox, *Ecclesiastes,* p. 3). The Hebrew word *kahal* gets translated into Greek as *ecclesia* and into English as "church." Thus in English we often refer to things having to do with a church as ecclesiastical. It should be obvious by now that the title of the book we call Ecclesiastes comes from the Greek of the first verse.

Ecclesiastes 12: 9, 10 further expounds the function of the Preacher. There we read that "in addition to being a wise man, the Preacher also taught the people knowledge; and he pondered, searched out and arranged many proverbs. The Preacher sought to find delightful words and to write words of truth correctly." His use of proverbs is evident throughout Ecclesiastes, especially in those sections that I labeled "words of advice" in my outline.

Ecclesiastes 1:1 also describes the Preacher as "the son of David, king in Jerusalem." And in verse 12 the Preacher claims to "have been king over Israel in Jerusalem." With such a description the name that comes to mind is that of Solomon, even though it shows up nowhere in the book. By way of contrast, the book of Proverbs starts out with "the proverbs of Solomon" (Prov. 1:1) and the Song of Solomon begins with "the Song of Songs, which is Solomon's" (S. of Sol. 1:1). For some reason Ecclesiastes avoids the name of Solomon. But up until modern times people generally equated the Preacher with him. Others, as we noted in the introduction, argue that the Preacher merely draws upon Solomon's experiences, especially in his opening discourses. Certainly no one in ancient Israel was more closely associated with wisdom and luxurious wealth than King Solomon. His experiences definitely illustrate the foolishness of seeking to gain meaning from earthly things.

Before moving on we need to note one additional thing about the author. The opening verses speak of the Preacher in the third person. We find the same thing in the book's closing section (12:9, 10). This has led some readers to see a second author as introducing the Preacher, whose words form the great core of the book, which uses the first person. But such a supposition is not necessary. After all, even modern authors often refer to their own works in the third person when discussing them in a formal preface. It appears that the Preacher chose to skillfully frame the body of his work by using the third person in speaking of himself.

But that is not what we find in much of Ecclesiastes. The first verse's claim that Ecclesiastes sets forth "the words of the Preacher" is echoed in such phrases as "I realized that this also" (1:17), "I said to myself" (2:15), and so on. It is important to recognize this point. In much of the book we are not dealing with God's thoughts, but with the opinions, comments, and observations of the frustrated Preacher whom God inspired to write in this probing format. It is important to note, therefore, that we need to weigh carefully the words of the Preacher before attempting to assign them doctrinal authority or to use them as guides for lifestyle.

One of the first things to strike people as they read Ecclesiastes is the

Preacher's claim that "all is vanity" (1:2). As we saw in the introduction, the word "vanity" is a translation of the Hebrew *hebel*, which literally means "vapor." And vapor, of course, has no substance. Scholars have used many English words to interpret *hebel*, but perhaps it is most accurately rendered as "absurd," "vain," or "meaningless."

No matter how we translate *hebel* the meaning is clear. And that clarity gets amplified by the five-fold repetition of *hebel* in verse 2: "'Vanity of vanities,' says the Preacher, 'Vanity of vanities! All is vanity.'" When Hebrew uses a word twice in succession it means the most that something can be. Thus the holy of holies is the most holy place and the king of kings is the most important king. The Preacher doesn't use *hebel* twice, but five times in one verse. His meaning is undeniable. "All" or everything is absolutely meaningless. That conclusion hints at

English Translation of *Hebel*

"Useless"—*Good News Bible*
"Emptiness"—*New English Bible*
"Meaningless"—New International Version
"Futile"—*Tanakh*
"Utterly vain"—*Moffatt*

what is to come in his book. *Hebel* reverberates down the corridors of Ecclesiastes. And the repetition of the superlative use of *hebel* in Ecclesiastes 12:8 reinforces the effect of the word. Thus the thought that everything is absolutely vain or absurd or meaningless provides the framework for the Preacher's thinking in the core of the book running from Ecclesiastes 1:3 to 12:8.

But, you may be thinking, *what does he mean when he says that "all is vanity"?* Does it, we need to ask, include godliness or God? If "all" includes those topics the Preacher would be desperately and profoundly out of harmony with the rest of the Bible.

Fortunately, the context supplies the meaning of "all" for the Preacher. Beginning in verse 3 he tells us plainly that he has in mind things "under the sun." Thus verse 2 read in context states that "everything under the sun is vanity." H. C. Leupold points out that "time and again the author presents what would normally have been regarded as a very extreme utterance, if not rank heresy. But the presence of the little phrase 'under the sun' always says in effect, 'What I claim is true if one deals with purely earthly values.'" "Each time the phrase occurs it is as though the author had said, 'Let us for the sake of argument momentarily rule out the higher things'" (Leupold, pp. 43, 42).

We must not interpret the Preacher's oft-repeated "under the sun" as being the sum total of what he sees as reality. He is quite explicit that "God is in heaven" while we "are on the earth" (Eccl. 5:2). In short, God and the things of God are "above the heavens." An "under the heavens" world is an existence without God and revelation from Him. In modern terms we would call it a secular world. In effect the Preacher tells us in verse 2 that everything is meaningless when evaluated only from a perspective that leaves God and His revelation out of the picture. Without the insight that comes from God, he is claiming, you can't really make sense of human life.

The French atheistic existentialist Albert Camus caught the spirit of the Preacher's frustration with earthly meaning in his *Myth of Sisyphus.* In Greek mythology the gods had condemned Sisyphus "forever to roll a stone up a hill in the lower world" (Hendricks, p. 319). The problem is that as soon as he pushes the large stone to the crest of the mountains it rolls back down, and he has to start over. As a result, Sisyphus's "whole being is exerted toward accomplishing nothing." The meaninglessness of the process, Camus notes, is still reflected in the absurd daily lives of people. He concludes that we need to find happiness in rolling our rock. After all, it is all we have (Camus, *Myth*, pp. 89-91).

The Preacher assumes the garb of secularity in a powerful demonstration that an "under the sun" understanding is not enough. His depiction begins in verse 3, in which he sets forth the rhetorical question of "What does man gain by all the toil at which he toils under the sun?" (RSV). The implied answer is "nothing."

> ## A Critique of Secularism
>
> "Qoheleth writes from concealed premises, and his book is in reality a major work of apologetic . . . theology. Its apparent worldliness is dictated by its aim: Qoheleth is addressing the general public whose view is bounded by the horizons of this world; he meets them on their own ground, and proceeds to convict them of its inherent vanity. . . . His book is in fact a critique of secularism and of secularized religion" (Hendry, p. 570).

He will drive that point home in the chapters that follow.

Meanwhile, we need to put ourselves in the place of the Preacher. "Perhaps if we are honest," suggests Robert Davidson, "we shall all find something of ourselves in him" (Davidson, p. 9). After all, don't we at times look at the world and conclude that it doesn't make sense? Don't we at times find the pat answers offered by even good church people to be less than adequate? And don't we in our down moments fear that the universe and our lives might have no ultimate meaning? Let's be honest here. If we are, we will find that Ecclesiastes is a book for our day.

Part II

Meaninglessness Demonstrated and Advice Given

Ecclesiastes 1:4–12:7

2. Meaninglessness in
the Endless Cycle of Nature

Ecclesiastes 1:3-11

*³What advantage does man have
    in all his work
Which he does under the sun?
⁴A generation goes and a genera-
    tion comes,
But the earth remains forever.
⁵ Also, the sun rises and the sun sets;
And hastening to its place it rises
    there again.
⁶Blowing toward the south,
Then turning toward the north,
The wind continues swirling
    along;
And on its circular courses the
    wind returns.
⁷All the rivers flow into the sea,
Yet the sea is not full.
To the place where the rivers flow,
There they flow again.
⁸All things are wearisome;
Man is not able to tell it.
The eye is not satisfied with
    seeing,
Nor is the ear filled with hearing.
⁹That which has been is that which*

> will be,
> And that which has been done is
>   that which will be done.
> So there is nothing new under the sun.
> [10]Is there anything of which one
>   might say,
> "See this, it is new"?
> Already it has existed for ages
> Which were before us.
> [11]There is no remembrance of ear-
>   lier things;
> And also of the later things
>   which will occur,
> There will be for them no
>   remembrance
> Among those who will come
>   later still.

Some people exuberantly jump out of bed in the morning, hardly able to contain their excitement for the challenges of a new day. But not everyone shares that spirit. Some only see each day as part of an endless grind, one day being pretty much a gray, dreary repetition of the previous infinite line of days. The Preacher represents the latter camp. Not only is each day dreary, it is also profitless (1:3).

We noted in section 1 that verse 3 with its pessimistic conclusion that life has no true lasting profit, no matter how hard one toils, provides a theme text that the Preacher will elaborate on in his next few chapters. His first demonstration of the profitlessness of life appears in verses 4-11, in which he deals with the ceaseless round, or cycles, of nature. Working within the context of verse 3, we might summarize the section by saying that if nothing ever changes, why struggle so hard to make a difference. After all, "there is nothing new under the sun" (verse 9) and even those things that one may have accomplished at the cost of much toil future generations will only forget (verse 11). The essence of verse 3 is that people spend their whole life working and end up with nothing to show for it.

Verse 4 picks up that pessimistic conclusion by noting that the generations come and go yet the earth remains forever. It's as if you and all your efforts have made no difference at all, that the sum total of your life's contribution is a big fat zero.

That lack of accomplishment is bad enough, but it gets worse. The generations come and go. In other words, you and I are born and die, yet "the earth remains." Jerome, the fourth century biblical scholar caught the irony in this observation, writing: "What is more vain than this vanity: that the earth, which was made for humans, stays—but humans themselves, the lords of the earth, suddenly dissolve into dust?" (in Crenshaw, *Ecclesiastes,* p. 63).

The Preacher hasn't actually mentioned the word "death" yet. But the transitoriness of human life is an issue that he will return to again and again. And to be absolutely frank, we all struggle with that one. I am just now at the point of retirement. I like the idea of not having to show up at the office. But I am not particularly looking forward to getting my tombstone. An "under the sun" existence just does not offer much hope.

Verses 5-7 amplify the meaninglessness of toil by three glimpses from creation.

- The sun rises and sets only to end up at where it began (verse 5).
- The wind blows south, then north, swirls around, and then does the whole thing over again (verse 6).
- The rivers run into the sea but accomplish nothing. The sea never fills up. The rivers face an eternal task but never accomplish it (verse 7).

Despite what appears to be constant change, it is really only an illusion. No real change ever takes place. Nor is there any rest for the sun, the wind, and the rivers. Only ceaseless toil, endless work that accomplishes nothing. This is truly *hebel*—meaninglessness, vanity, absurdity.

That thought brings us to the discouraging conclusion of verse 8: "All things are wearisome." Or as the Good News Translation puts it, "everything leads to weariness—a weariness too great for words." The ongoing cycles of nature without accomplishment leave the Preacher feeling totally discouraged, dissatisfied beyond words.

What a difference perspective makes. To the psalmist the heavens declared the glory of God. The sun on its daily circuit appeared to him as "a strong man" running "its course with joy" (Ps. 19:1, 5, RSV).

Michael Eaton points out that the Preacher's "under the sun" viewpoint contrasts markedly with that of Old Testament believers, "who loved creation and saw in it the majesty of God's name, looked with admiration at the skies, pondered the lessons taught by animals, wind, grass and trees, and sang to the glory of God because of" what they saw and heard. "The Preacher's point is that all this is lost in an 'under the sun' viewpoint; all that is left is nature in a state of exhaustion" (Eaton, p. 59).

We find a vital lesson here. How we think determines what we see and how we interpret it. A vast difference exists between an "under the sun" perspective and an "above the sun" understanding.

The Preacher's pessimism at the end of verse 8 compares the human situation to that of the endless, fruitless rounds, or cycles, of nature, when he points out that "the eye is not satisfied with seeing, nor is the ear filled with hearing." "Like the ocean, our senses are fed and fed, but never filled. . . . The journey goes on; we never arrive" (Kidner, *Message*, pp. 25, 26).

> Life from the perspective of the Preacher is like the little boy on his rocking horse. He had lots of motion but no progress.

That thought brings us to verses 9 and 10 and the conclusion that "there is nothing new under the sun," that is, what will be has already been, and that which will be done in the future has already been done in the past (verse 9). Even when people think they have something new they have nothing but an illusion, since that which they mistakenly regard as new already existed in previous generations (verse 10).

Now we should point out that the Preacher undoubtedly knew that some new things do happen even from an "under the sun" perspective. After all, the current president of the United States has never been president before. Likewise, the fact that your oldest son got married on his twenty-fourth birthday had never happened to him in the past. The Preacher was well aware of those sorts of unique events. "He was not claiming that specific historical events recur, but rather that all *types* of events (wars, say, or natural disasters) recur, and therefore nothing that happens can be fundamentally new" (Fox, *Ecclesiastes*, pp. 6, 7).

In such a cyclical view of history the Preacher stands over against the historical perspective set forth by both the Old Testament prophets and the writers of the New Testament. To them history is not merely a closed circuit going nowhere but around and around endlessly. To the contrary, for other Bible writers history has a destination— history is in the flow of time that extends from the Fall of Adam to the coming of the Messiah and on to the Second Advent.

An "under the sun" understanding is totally different from a perspective informed by God's revelations from heaven. But the Preacher hasn't taken us that far yet. He first needs to tear down hope in all strictly human effort and machinations. Only after he has his readers thoroughly discouraged and hopeless will he introduce us to his view of the good news about God's justice in his last few verses.

Meanwhile, he will continue to lead us in verse 11 in an "under the sun" posture. There he tells us that things won't change in the future. Just as the present generation does not remember previous accomplishments, so our successors will forget what we have managed to do. So much for meaning in the great cycle of life as the Preacher drives one last nail into its coffin.

And so much for an "under the sun" view of creation and history. It is an important perspective. What appears to be the one certain allusion in the New Testament to Ecclesiastes comes from its first chapter. Romans 8:20 tells us that "the creation" has been "subjected to futility" (RSV). But Romans doesn't leave it there. It has the creation eagerly longing for a better day (verse 19).

That better day, of course, began at the first coming of Christ and will reach fullness at His second advent. David Hubbard puts us in contact with that more hopeful view of history when he writes that "Jesus entered our history to teach us to remember and hope. He pointed to a past worth recalling in his death and resurrection; he depicted a future worth anticipating in his church and his return. . . . Futile days and futile weeks we may have, where life loses its glue and turns leaky at the seams. But a futile life will not be our lot. Christ's news is too good to let that happen. Life is filled with meaning because he is making all things new—beginning with us" (Hubbard, *Ecclesiastes,* p. 55).

3. Meaninglessness in Human Wisdom

Ecclesiastes 1:12-18

¹²I, the Preacher, have been king over Israel in Jerusalem. ¹³And I set my mind to seek and explore by wisdom concerning all that has been done under heaven. It is a grievous task which God has given to the sons of men to be afflicted with. ¹⁴I have seen all the works which have been done under the sun, and behold, all is vanity and striving after wind. ¹⁵What is crooked cannot be straightened and what is lacking cannot be counted.

¹⁶I said to myself, "Behold, I have magnified and increased wisdom more than all who were over Jerusalem before me; and my mind has observed a wealth of wisdom and knowledge." ¹⁷And I set my mind to know wisdom and to know madness and folly; I realized that this also is striving after wind. ¹⁸Because in much wisdom there is much grief, and increasing knowledge results in increasing pain.

Those of us who enjoy the life of the intellect will not consider this passage good news. But then good news is rather a rare commodity in Ecclesiastes.

"After the pessimism of 1:2-11," Michael Eaton observes, "the following sections shut off all escape routes" for those who want to solve all their problems with an "under the sun" approach (Eaton, p. 61). Verses 12-18 tell us that human wisdom only makes life more painful, the first 11 verses of chapter 2 help us see that pleasure does not hold the answer, and then Ecclesiastes 2:12-17 inform us that the only real certainty in life is death.

In our present passage we find the Preacher shifting into high gear as he begins to relentlessly drive home his thesis that everything is meaningless (1:2) and that no matter how much energy one expends it will not produce anything worthwhile (1:3). Up through Ecclesiastes 1:11 he has demonstrated his thesis in an impressionistic sort of way by picturing the world as endlessly busy but only going in circles. Now in verses 12-18 he sharpens the focus. He turns from impressions and analogies to those things that we can know from experience.

The first installment in the Preacher's contribution to our advanced understanding of the utter futility of human existence has to do with wisdom. And what better example of that test can there be than the person of King Solomon himself, who appears to be in mind even though verse 12 does not name him. He was notorious for his wisdom, according to the historical books of the Bible.

The saga begins when God asked the young king what he would like to have as a divine endowment. "Give thy servant . . . an understanding mind" he replied (1 Kings 3:5, 9, RSV).

God's response was an enthusiastic yes to the king's request. "Behold, I give you a wise and discerning mind, so that none like you has been before you and none like you shall arise after you" (verse 12, RSV).

Later in his reign the Bible tells us that "Solomon's wisdom surpassed the wisdom of all the sons of the east, and all the wisdom of Egypt. For he was wiser than all men" (1 Kings 4:30, 31). When the queen of Sheba heard of his wisdom "she came to test him with difficult questions." After Solomon successfully answered "all her questions, . . . she said to the king, 'It was a true report which I heard in my own land about your words and your wisdom.'" In actual fact, she noted, he was much wiser than even what people had told her (1 Kings 10:1, 3, 6, 7).

Solomon was the very personification of wisdom in the Old Testament. There is no better example. It is against that backdrop that the Preacher's pronouncements on wisdom take on their full significance.

In Ecclesiastes 1:13 he informs us that he made a conscious decision to put wisdom to the test—"to seek and explore by wisdom concerning all that has been done under heaven." But surprise of surprises, he discovered that the experiment didn't work out as smoothly as he had anticipated. In fact, it turned out to be "grievous" and even a painful task (verse 14, 18).

Here we find a conclusion that should catch the eye of those familiar with the book of Proverbs. There we read:

"Happy is the man who finds wisdom,
and the man who gets understanding,
for the gain from it is better than gain from silver
and its profit better than gold.
She is more precious than jewels,
and nothing you desire can compare with her.
Long life is in her right hand;
in her left hand are riches and honor.
Her ways are ways of pleasantness,
and all her paths are peace.
She is a tree of life to those who lay hold of her;
those who hold her fast are called happy"
(Prov. 3:13-18, RSV).

Ecclesiastes reaches quite a different conclusion. It appears that even good things have their downside. Perhaps a better way to put it is that even they have their limitations. We must never forget what the Preacher is trying to demonstrate. His aim is to arrive at satisfactory truth by relying solely on human knowledge—"under heaven" knowledge (Eccl. 1:13), "under the sun" knowledge. His conclusion regarding that method: Not only doesn't it work, it is like trying to catch the wind (verse 17).

In order to drive the futility of human wisdom home, the Preacher sets forth his points in a deliberate manner.

A. First he introduces himself in verse 12.
B. Next he provides an account of his quest for understanding in the first half of verse 13.
C. Then in the last part of verse 13 and in verse 14 he offers a negative summary of his findings.
D. Last, he sets forth a proverb confirming his discoveries in verse 15.

The important thing to note is that verses 16-18 basically provide a repetition of verses 12-15. Note the similarities:

A^1. First, the Preacher provides a personal introduction in verse 16.
B^1. Next he provides an account of his quest for understanding in the

first half of verse 17.

C¹. Then in the last part of verse 17 he offers a negative summary of his findings.

D¹. Last, he sets forth a proverb confirming his discoveries in verse 18.

And why, you may be thinking, *did he basically repeat himself in a few short verses?* For the same reason that he multiplied his use of "vanity" when he asserted "vanity of vanities! All is vanity" (1:2). His repetition is a deliberate literary device used to drive his point home, to leave his readers without doubt concerning his conclusions.

And what were they? First, human wisdom turned out to be just one more avenue to vanity or futility. The Preacher describes its effectiveness with the vivid phrase "striving after wind" (2:14, 17), an often used saying in Ecclesiastes, but not found elsewhere in the Old Testament. Trying to catch the wind is a word picture that we can easily visualize. We may think we are about to grasp it, only to discover that it has slipped through our fingers. And if you finally caught a handful of wind, what would you have? Such says the Preacher is the fruit of human wisdom.

A second conclusion is that human wisdom cannot make the crooked straight or count that which does not exist (verse 15). "There are twists *(what is crooked)* and gaps *(what is lacking)* in all thinking. No matter how the thinker ponders, he cannot straighten out life's anomalies, nor reduce all he sees to a neat system. . . . Frustration and perplexity surround the philosopher. His wisdom may help in some things, but it cannot solve the fundamental problem of life" (Eaton, p. 63). Wisdom cannot change reality. It can diagnose its ills but is helpless when it comes to resolving life's greatest perplexities.

A third conclusion is that "in much wisdom there is much grief, and increasing knowledge results in increasing pain" (verse 18). It is not the lack of wisdom but its presence that troubled the Preacher. He had found what he was searching for but it proved futile. Even worse than that, it was painful. The further he explores, the greater his perplexity. "In the end," Robert Davidson asserts, "he is left facing a mystery which he is no nearer solving than when he set out. For all his knowledge, he is no nearer discovering the ultimate meaning of life" (Davidson, p. 14).

In my own personal struggles for meaning I have come to similar conclusions. Knowledge to me is like working your way through a funnel backwards. The further you go the more there is to know and the more complicated and perplexing life seems to be. The modern saying "ignorance is bliss" captures in part the Preacher's meaning. To be frank, life has some things that it is better not to know.

Several decades ago, after struggling with the problems I was aware of in the church and facing what seemed to me to be the false promises of Christianity, I resigned from the ministry and decided to find another way through life. My route was a doctorate in philosophy. But I ran into a problem. After six years I discovered that philosophy was bankrupt when it came to real answers. That conclusion was the goad that began to drive me back to a genuine Christianity.

The apostle Paul sums up the problems we face on earth when he writes that in this present world "we see through a glass, darkly" (1 Cor. 13:12, KJV). The Preacher's glass in Ecclesiastes was particularly dark because it left out the explanatory power of divine revelation.

But the good news is that there is a "wisdom from above" that is "without uncertainty or insincerity" (James 3:17, RSV). That wisdom is centered in Jesus of Nazareth. The Queen of Sheba may have come "from the ends of the earth to hear the wisdom of Solomon" but we can say of Jesus that "something greater than Solomon is here" (Matt. 12:42).

Human wisdom may be lacking in answers and solutions—it may be the way of pain and futility in the face of life's real problems—but there exists an above the sun wisdom that is indeed "a tree of life to those who lay hold of her" (Prov. 3:18, RSV).

4. Meaninglessness in Pleasure and Wealth

Ecclesiastes 2:1-11

> *¹I said to myself, "Come now, I will test you with pleasure. So enjoy yourself." And behold, it too was futility. ²I said of laughter, "It is madness," and of pleasure, "What does it accomplish?" ³I explored with my mind how to stimulate my body with wine while my mind was guiding me wisely, and how to take hold of folly, until I could see what good there is for the sons of men to do under heaven the few years of their lives. ⁴I enlarged my works: I built houses for myself, I planted vineyards for myself; ⁵I made gardens and parks for myself and I planted in them all kinds of fruit trees; ⁶I made ponds of water for myself from which to irrigate a forest of growing trees. ⁷I bought male and female slaves and I had homeborn slaves. Also I possessed flocks and herds larger than all who preceded me in Jerusalem. ⁸Also, I collected for myself silver and gold and the treasure of kings and provinces. I provided for myself male and female singers and the pleasures of men—many concubines.*
>
> *⁹Then I became great and increased more than all who preceded me in Jerusalem. My wisdom also stood by me. ¹⁰All that my eyes desired I did not refuse them. I did not withhold my heart from any pleasure, for my heart was pleased because of all my labor and this was my reward for all my labor. ¹¹Thus I considered all my activities which my hands had done and the labor which I had exerted, and behold all was vanity and striving after wind and there was no profit under the sun.*

We have all felt it sometime. "If I only had that new house my life would be complete." "If I just had that better car I could truly be happy." "If only I had . . ."

But for some of us it is not possessions. "If I could only do" is our cry.

"If I could only be the most successful salesperson." "If I could only be an Olympic champion." More personally, "If I could only write one more book." "If I could only" is the driving force of our lives.

All of us live on the "if only I" level some of the time. For others of us it is a full time location. The Preacher takes up that approach to ultimate meaning in Ecclesiastes 2:1-11. A probing thinker, he is still working on the great question he raised in the third verse of chapter 1: "What does a man gain by all the toil at which he toils under the sun?" (RSV). Having just finished trying human wisdom as the answer, he discovered that it was as satisfying as chasing after the wind (1:17). In the end it provided more pain than fulfillment (1:18). But our friend the Preacher, to say the least, is a man of perseverance. He hinted at the next stage of his journey when he told us he was not only going to experiment with wisdom but also with "madness and folly" (1:17). That is, he will cover the entire range of human experiences in his search for true meaning and purpose.

In Ecclesiastes 2:1 he shifts his quest to pleasure and wealth to discover whether they held the key to life's purpose. Once again Solomon's life and experience offers the very best example possible. As Kathleen Farmer notes, "Someone like Solomon, who could be said to have done almost anything he wanted to do and to have possessed everything his eyes and his heart desired, makes a convincing witness to the ultimate lack of satisfaction such things give to the one who has them" (Farmer, p. 157). The title of Harold Kushner's book on Ecclesiastes, *When All You've Ever Wanted Isn't Enough,* is an apt summary of Ecclesiastes.

As usual, the Preacher puts his conclusions right up front in verse 2. He discovered two things.

1. The result of the lighter side of pleasure is "madness,"
2. and the more serious side achieves nothing substantial.

The New Living Translation helpfully renders verse 2 as " 'it is silly to be laughing all the time,' I said. 'What good does it do to seek only pleasure?' "

The Preacher tells us in no uncertain terms in verse 3 that he "explored with my mind." That is a crucial point that will come up again in verse 9, in which he notes that "my wisdom also stood by me." "He is *not,*" Robert Davidson points out, "advocating mindless debauchery. You would never have found him drunk and incapable or among the helpless heroin addicts. In all that he does he is determined to remain in self-control." Thus he might "seek the stimulus of wine, . . . but never be its victim. This is an experiment. He wants to see whether it works" (Davidson, p. 15).

Another item to note in verse 3 is the observation about the few short years a person has to find meaning. The specter of death, as we will see repeatedly, never wanders far from the Preacher's mind. The grave is always lurking around the corner, ready to extinguish whatever meaning we might have discovered.

Verses 4-6 list the Preacher's splendid accomplishments. The first thing that jumps off the page is the egocentricity of the search. In the words of the King James Version:

> "I made me . . ." (verse 4).
> "I builded me . . ." (verse 4).
> "I planted me . . ." (verse 4).
> "I made me . . ." (verse 5).
> "I made me . . ." (verse 6).
> "I got me . . ." (verse 7).
> "I gathered me . . ." (verse 8).
> "I gat me . . ." (verse 8).

The rather "modest" conclusion after all those statements is that "I became great" (verse 9). Such self-centeredness, C. L. Seow observes, is much like "similar lists in the royal inscriptions elsewhere in the ancient Near East" (Seow, p. 128). We observe it in King Nebuchadnezzar's brag: "Is not this great Babylon, which I have built by my mighty power as a royal residence and for the glory of my majesty?" (Dan. 4:30, RSV).

At any rate, we find ourselves dealing with a person who has it all—has all the marks of earthly success and all the possessions one could possibly desire. And such was King Solomon, the individual who represented the apex not only of Israel's wisdom, but also of its wealth. For all the magnificence of the Temple, we read in 1 Kings 7:1 that it took him 13 years to finish his own palace, nearly twice as long as he spent constructing the house of God.

And beyond the palace, he built himself the House of the Forest of Lebanon (verse 2), the Hall of Pillars (verse 6), the Hall of Judgment (verse 7), and other buildings. "All of these were made of costly stones, hewn according to measure" and cedar (verses 9-12, RSV).

Song of Songs 8:11 alludes to Solomon's fabled vineyard, and gardens and parks (see Eccl. 2:5) are one of the traditional marks of rulers (and any others rich enough to afford them) all the way from the hanging gardens of Babylon up through the French kings and into the present day. In the ancient world such royal parks had both aesthetic and practical value, providing both shade and delicious fruit. They also tended to be places for royal sport and a handy source of wild game. And in Nehemiah 2:8 we find the king's enclosed park a source of timber for building a defensive wall around the city of Jerusalem.

Ecclesiastes also represents the king as making ponds for irrigation (2:6). Once again, this was a royal necessity in a land with neither major rivers nor adequate rainfall. Thus we find Mesha, king of Moab, claiming not only to have built cities but also that "I made both of its reservoirs for water inside the town" (Pritchard, p. 320). The Bible notes such accomplishments in both Nehemiah's day and in that of Hezekiah (Neh. 2:14; 2 Kings 18:17).

The book of Ecclesiastes depicts Solomon as being the richest of the rich. He not only had a lot of improved real estate in Ecclesiastes 2:4-6, but verse 7 tells us that he had more than adequate numbers of slaves, flocks, and herds. No one, Scripture declares, had outdone Solomon in such possessions. We read in 1 Kings 4:22, 23 that the king's table daily required vast amounts of fine flour and meal, 10 fat oxen, 20 cattle, 100 sheep, along with harts, gazelles, roebucks, and fatted fowl. He wasn't short of things to satiate his appetite or entertain his senses. And then, of course, he had an adequate supply of women—"the pleasures of men" (Eccl. 2:8). Commentators debate the exact meaning of the phrase, but most modern interpreters agree that it is alluding to concubines. At any rate, Scripture elsewhere represents Solomon as having more than enough to go around—700 wives and 300 concubines (1 Kings 11:1-3). Even if some of those were political relationships, most monogamists would agree that he was well cared for in the "pleasures of men" category. And if he was short on anything he had massive amounts of slaves and gold to buy more (Eccl. 2:8; 1 Kings 10:14-25). According to 2 Chronicles 9:27 "the king made silver as common in Jerusalem as stone" (RSV).

The point of all this catalog: to demonstrate that here is a person who had it all in terms of both wealth and pleasure. If anybody could find meaning in such things it should have been him.

In our day such a person would probably be into oil in a big way or the CEO of one of the world's great businesses. A modern equivalent of Solomon would have a villa on the Riviera, a fabulous chalet in Switzerland, and vacation mansions on various islands of the world. Such a person would be a patron of the arts and would most certainly have all of his or her pleasures satisfied. They would be the envy of multitudes.

But would it have meaning? Do such things really make life worth-while? That is the Preacher's question. And he answers it in Ecclesiastes 2:9-11. At first the answer looks positive. He became not just great but the greatest (verse 9), and he certainly enjoyed his pleasure. This was his "re-ward" (verse 10).

But when he sat down to think it over he concluded that the way of pleasure and possessions was nothing but meaninglessness, a chasing after the wind, a profitless enterprise (verse 11). When he looked back and evaluated all of these things he discovered that they did not hold the answer to meaning. He ended up sort of like an ancient Donald Trump, who wrote that "my attention span is short, and probably my least favorite thing to do is to maintain the status quo. Instead of being content when everything is going fine, I start getting impatient and irritable. For me the important thing is the getting, not the having" (quoted in Hubbard, *Ecclesiastes,* p. 77).

The Problem with Pleasure

"Pleasure satisfies only during the act. Repetition is the key to pleasure. One drink, one sexual fling, one contest won, one project accomplished, one wild party—none of these, nor all of them put together, can be enough to bring satisfaction. The quest for pleasure is like eating salted peanuts; it is impossible to stop after the first bite. One bite leads to another because the first leaves no lasting impact. To reflect on the delights of the first peanut is far less gratifying than to reach for the second. Far from comforting us, each act of pleasure leaves us thirsty for the next" (Hubbard, *Ecclesiastes,* p. 77).

The Preacher, like so many down through history, had run up against the "'paradox of hedonism,' . . . the more you hunt for pleasure, the less of it you find" (Kidner, *Message,* p. 31). And, we might add, the bigger and bigger dose you need to maintain even moderate pleasure. The Preacher summarizes it nicely later in his book when he writes that "he who loves money will not be satisfied with money" (5:10, RSV).

The Preacher claims to have gotten a reward but no profit. He means that he found enjoyment in what he did but that such passing pleasure did not make life meaningful. Iain Provan puts it succinctly when he writes that "there is no surplus to joy beyond joy itself" (Provan, p. 79). It takes more than sensual pleasure and accomplishment, the Preacher declares, to give life true meaning. Like him, the apostle Paul concluded that all of his accomplishments (even religious attainments) were no better than "dung" (Phil. 3:4-8, KJV).

The Preacher and Paul, along with us, begin to find the secret of meaning in the words of Jesus: "If you try to keep your life for yourself, you will lose it. But if you give up your life for me, you will find true life. And how do you benefit if you gain the whole world but lose or forfeit your own soul in the process?" (Luke 9:24, 25, NLT).

5. Meaninglessness in the Face of Death

Ecclesiastes 2:12-17

¹²So I turned to consider wisdom, madness and folly; for what will the man do who will come after the king except what has already been done? ¹³And I saw that wisdom excels folly as light excels darkness. ¹⁴The wise man's eyes are in his head, but the fool walks in darkness. And yet I know that one fate befalls them both. ¹⁵Then I said to myself, "As is the fate of the fool, it will also befall me. Why then have I been extremely wise?" So I said to myself, "This too is vanity." ¹⁶For there is no lasting remembrance of the wise man as with the fool, inasmuch as in the coming days all will be forgotten. And how the wise man and the fool alike die! ¹⁷So I hated life, for the work which had been done under the sun was grievous to me; because everything is futility and striving after wind.

The person who dies with the most toys wins," reads the bumper sticker. Better yet is the one that declares, "The person with the most toys still dies."

The Preacher, from his under the sun perspective, would have agreed with both bumper stickers. But he would have found the second to be utterly frustrating.

The problem of death looms large throughout Ecclesiastes. It is always lurking around some corner, waiting to rip away any advantages or rewards a person might have gained through wisdom or toil.

The Preacher wasn't the only person in the ancient world to be concerned with death. The great pyramids of Egypt indicate that the issue of death dominated the lives of the pharaohs. That of Pharaoh Khufu rises about 500 feet above the desert floor and consists of some 2,300,000 blocks of stone, each weighing two tons or more. While Napoleon's generals climbed to its top, the emperor rested below, calculating that the stones in the three greatest pyramids would build a wall 10 feet high and one foot thick around the entire nation of France. The rulers of Egypt were desperate in the face of death. The pyramids themselves were not only tombs but aids to help them arrive at their heavenly home.

In Ecclesiastes 2:12-17 the Preacher continues to struggle with the meaning of life. He returns to his meditations on wisdom and folly, in which he includes "not only the 'madness' of self-indulgence and cynicism but the pursuit of pleasure" at all levels (Kidner, *Message*, pp. 33, 34). Testing both of them in Ecclesiastes 1:12-2:11, he found that they both fall short of helping him discover true meaning. Turning to them again in Ecclesiastes 2:12, he asks, "What will the man do who will come after the king except what has already been done?"

The idea seems to be in that very controverted passage that if Solomon with all of his wisdom and wealth couldn't use them to discover the meaning of life, then what hope could any lesser mortal possibly have?

Verse 13 begins a comparison of the merits of wisdom and folly, with the Preacher definitely concluding that wisdom was superior to folly, just as much as "light excels darkness." Here the Preacher agrees with traditional wisdom. Wisdom is like the gift of light for a person walking. It enables one to avoid costly mistakes and stumbles. Duane Garrett puts it aptly when he writes that "the wise know where they are going, even if they only know they are heading for trouble. They therefore can avoid some disasters and be prepared for others. Fools, however, are always surprised by events that befall them" (Garrett, p. 294).

The first part of Ecclesiastes 2:14 continues the light and darkness contrast of verse 13. "The wise man's eyes," we read, "are in his head, but the fool walks in darkness," thereby inviting disaster.

Here again the Preacher echoes other wisdom writers. Proverbs characterizes the fool as one who "does not delight in understanding" (Prov. 18:2) and finds wickedness to be like a sport (10:23). Therefore, we read in Proverbs 4:18, 19 that

> "The path of the righteous is like the
> light of dawn,

> That shines brighter and brighter until
>   the full day.
> The way of the wicked is like darkness;
> They do not know over what they stumble."

The New Testament presents the same picture. Jesus tells us that sinners love darkness (John 3:19) and Paul refers to them as darkness itself (Eph. 5:8).

So far so good in the Preacher's comparison of wisdom and folly. "For a brief moment," writes David Hubbard, "it looks as if the quest has come to its 'Eureka!' its grand 'Aha!' It sounds as though the guiding question of 1:3 has found its satisfying answer: There is profit for the human toil of delving into life's mysteries. *'Wisdom'* is the answer. We stand ready to applaud the outcome, watch the curtain drop, and cheer the Preacher as he takes his final bows" (Hubbard, *Ecclesiastes,* p. 84).

But then comes the second half of verse 14 with its devastating conclusion that the same fate awaits both the wise and the foolish. Both alike die (verse 16). Therefore wisdom is useless as a cure for life's ultimate problem. Death mocks human achievement.

At this point we need to realize that from the Preacher's under the sun perspective the grave is the end of the line. Death is the great unknown from which there is no escape (3:19-21). From him we find no assurance of another life. "For Qoheleth . . . the tree has withered and died. The seemingly black-and-white contrast between wisdom and folly dissolves into a sea of gray before the indiscriminate reality of death. Whether sage or fool, king or commoner, all must succumb to the great equalizer and cross the threshold into the democracy of the dead" (Brown, p. 35).

But that seems all wrong. "All our lives" Hubbard observes, "we have been taught that wisdom pays, that prudence succeeds, that knowledge wins. And then comes death to undo all that we have learned. No final hope can be found in wisdom, because death outlasts it" (Hubbard, *Beyond Futility,* p. 43).

That irrefutable fact leads the Preacher to question why he had spent so much time and energy seeking to be "extremely wise," since the entire attempt turns out to be *hebel,* "meaninglessness," in the face of death (Eccl. 2:15).

With deliverance from death not an option, the Preacher, in traditional Jewish fashion, at least expected an enduring remembrance of his reputation. That might not be as good as life, but it has some value.

The apocryphal book of Ecclesiasticus helps us grasp the importance of the remembrance of the dead in Jewish society.

> "The human body is a fleeting thing,
>> but a virtuous name will never be blotted out.
> Have regard for your name, since it will outlive
>> you longer than a thousand hoards of gold.
> The days of a good life are numbered,
>> but a good name lasts forever"
>> (41:11-13, NRSV).

On the other side of the issue, one of the curses against the wicked in the book of Psalms is that "his name [might] be blotted out in the second generation" (Ps. 109:13, RSV).

The injustice of death itself gets compounded for the Preacher, who declares that "there is no lasting remembrance of the wise man" or the fool, "inasmuch as in the coming days all will be forgotten" (Eccl. 2:16). How can this be? he wails at the end of verse 16. How is it that wisdom counts for nothing, not even remembrance beyond the grave?

"So I hated life," he exclaims in a fit of bitterness, "for the work which had been done under the sun was grievous to me; because everything is futility and striving after wind" (2:17). If no hope exists, why try? Why not just enjoy the life of a fool and get it over with? Why exert one's mind in a life that ends in utter nothingness, not even remembrance? The Preacher began his book claiming that life was absurd. If he started in the hole of despair, his searchings in the first two chapters have only made his pit deeper and more hopeless. "I hated life" is strong language for a wisdom teacher, who belonged to a profession aimed at finding the secrets of a long life. The personification of wisdom in Proverbs 8:35 declares that "he who finds me finds life." But from the Preacher's under the sun perspective death is the end of the line for both the wise and the foolish. He cannot see beyond the grave.

Other Old Testament writers show their concern with death. But none see it in such stark terms as Ecclesiastes.

In Psalm 49, for example, we read that both the fool and the wise die and that the foolish will find their homes in the grave. "But," claims the psalmist, "God will ransom my soul from the power of Sheol, for he will receive me" (Ps. 49:10-15, RSV). Here is a hope beyond the grasp of the Preacher in Ecclesiastes 2:15-17.

The New Testament fleshes out that hope. Jesus proclaims His victory over death and the grave (Rev. 1:18), a victory that He wants to share with those wise in the way of salvation. The above the sun hope of the gospel is that "death" will be "swallowed up in victory" at the end of time as those who have accepted Christ rise from the grave (1 Cor. 15:51-55, RSV).

The Preacher had it right from an earthly perspective. Neither the foolish nor the wise have any hope. But that is not the only viewpoint. The Preacher knows that. He will close his book on a different note. But first he needs to bring us with himself to the pit of despair. Then and only then will we be able to fully appreciate the magnitude of what God has in store for those who are truly wise in an above the sun fashion.

6. Meaninglessness of Toil

Ecclesiastes 2:18-23

[18] Thus I hated all the fruit of my labor for which I had labored under the sun, for I must leave it to the man who will come after me. [19] And who knows whether he will be a wise man or a fool? Yet he will have control over all the fruit of my labor for which I have labored by acting wisely under the sun. This too is vanity. [20] Therefore I completely despaired of all the fruit of my labor for which I had labored under the sun. [21] When there is a man who has labored with wisdom, knowledge and skill, then he gives his legacy to one who has not labored with them. This too is vanity and a great evil. [22] For what does a man get in all his labor and in his striving with which he labors under the sun? [23] Because all his days his task is painful and grievous; even at night his mind does not rest. This too is vanity.

Some years ago a book titled *On the Line* examined the experience of workers on factory assembly lines. One of the findings was that normal people considered such work meaningless. It did not challenge their minds or let them use their individual talents. In fact, an important discovery was that those who were mentally deficient were more efficient in an assembly line than those in the normal range. Normal people often made their day (or work) meaningful by inventing little ways to sabotage the product in some manner.

All of us want meaning. And we want it in our work. After all, that is what we do for most of our day for most of our life. And if you hate life (see Eccl. 2:17) it is probable that it is related to your work (verse 18). It is the word "hate" that ties Ecclesiastes 2:12-17 to 2:18-23.

The Revised Standard Version's rendering of verse 18 is helpful as we begin to unpack the meaning of our passage: "I hated all my toil in which I had toiled under the sun." "Toil" or "labor" is translated from the Hebrew *'āmāl* and is one of several Hebrew words used for work and its synonyms, with *'āmāl* relating "to the dark side of labor, the grievous and unfulfilling aspect of work" (Harris, vol. II, p. 675). *'Āmāl* appears 16 times in the Hebrew Bible, with 13 of them in Ecclesiastes, the tone being set in the opening verses with the Preacher asking "what advantage does man have in all his work . . . ?" (1:3). *'Āmāl*, as we see in our present passage, is not only used of labor and toil "but also the results" of labor, "the product or fruit of labor" (VanGemeren, vol. 3, p. 436). The real target of the Preacher's hatred in Ecclesiastes 2:18 is not his wealth but the labor he invested in obtaining it. And for most of Ecclesiastes it is not the toiling itself that bothers him but the fact that it fails to achieve a profit—a lasting benefit or accomplishment (1:3). Death, of course, cuts off everything he might have gained, as we saw in Ecclesiastes 2:12-17. The Preacher does have some positive things to say about *'āmāl* in other places. He says, for example, that "it is God's gift to man that every one should eat and drink and take pleasure in all his toil" (3:13, RSV). But, as Michael Fox points out, "toil is a source of pleasure only insofar as it provides the means of pleasure" (Fox, *A Time to Tear Down,* p. 100).

The concept of pleasure from toil is a million miles from the thoughts of the Preacher in chapter 2. Whatever one might have gained in life, he reported in verse 12-17, gets cut short by death.

But death itself is not the final aspect of meaninglessness related to toil. The Preacher hates the fruits of his labor because they won't even be his to enjoy, but his heir will inherit them (verse 18). And that conclusion raises two more absurdities in the Preacher's mind. First, the heir may be a fool (verse 19). And even if he is not a fool, he will have made no personal investment in the property. He gets the pleasure of enjoying it while all the toiler receives is a grave. How stupid can life get? is the thrust of the Preacher's conclusions.

At this point he is about as worked up as a philosopher can get. Just look at the words he employs to express his feelings of utter depression. First, *"I hated"* (verse 18), as we noted above, not only connects the passage with verses 12-17, it sets the tone for verses 18-23. Second, *"who knows*" (verse 19), David Hubbard observes, "rings with the frustration not of gray uncertainty but of black certainty" (Hubbard, *Ecclesiastes,* p. 89). The rhetorical question "who knows" occurs 10 times in the Old Testament, four of them in Ecclesiastes (2 Sam. 12:22; Joel 2:14; Jonah 3:9; Ps. 90:11; Esther 4:14; Prov. 24:22; and Eccl. 2:19; 3:21; 6:12; 8:1). In five of those texts the question leaves open the possibility of a positive answer, but not in Ecclesiastes. For the preacher it "expresses utter skepticism" (Crenshaw, *Ecclesiastes,* p. 87). Third, "vanity" or "meaningless" (verses 19, 21, 23). The threefold use of *hebel* in these few verses drives home the utter absurdity of the results of a person's life work. Fourth, *"I completely despaired"* (verse 20) highlights the Preacher's sense of hopelessness. Fifth, "a great evil" (verse 21) lines up with the rest of the Preacher's valuations and amplifies them. And sixth, the toil-related triumvirate of *"striving"* (verse 22), *"painful"* (verse 23), and *"grievous"* (verse 23) round out the setting of a mood reflecting total depression. We are truly dealing with a person who had come, temporarily at least, to the place where he could say with all sincerity that he hated both life (verse 17) and the fruit of his work (verse 18).

> ## Thoughts on Ecclesiastes 2:18-23
>
> "No biblical passage paints a grimmer picture of what it costs to succeed on human terms and how fragile that success is. . . . Strain, toil, pain, vexation, insomnia—this is the currency with which we pay for success that we can neither truly gain nor keep" (Hubbard, *Beyond Futility,* p. 44).

It wouldn't have been so bad if the Preacher hadn't tried so hard, if he hadn't put so much energy and mental effort into his work. The root words for "toil", "work," or "labor" appear nine times in the six verses running from 18 to 23. The Preacher was not casual about his work. It was serious to him—he had put his mind and his whole being into his toil. Not only does the Preacher claim to have acted "wisely" (verse 19), but according to verse 21 he "labored with wisdom, knowledge and skill." More than merely putting forth average effort, he found himself "striving" in his work (verse 22), so much so that he found it difficult to sleep because of his obsession with it (verse 23).

We are not dealing with a moderate approach to toil in these verses.

Rather, we have here one who threw his whole self into his work. But having put his life into it, he is all the more frustrated with the ultimate results of earthly toil.

All those years of wise and energetic labor and what does he get? A death after which he will be forgotten (verses 12-17). That is bad enough, but the very thought of leaving all he has achieved to someone else is almost more than he can tolerate, especially if that person is a fool who doesn't know how to appreciate what he has inherited or how to build upon, strengthen, and extend it.

The Bible nowhere mentions Solomon's son Rehoboam in connection with such a fear, but he certainly makes a good illustration of the point. His father had expanded the kingdom of Israel to its highest point, but the son who inherited it alienated 10 of the nation's tribes through his foolish arrogance and permanently divided the country into two nations—Judah in the south and Israel in the north (1 Kings 11:41-12:24). As James Crenshaw points out, Rehoboam's "folly was the subject of ridicule in the official story that circulated in the southern kingdom" (Crenshaw, *Ecclesiastes*, p. 87).

Every truly wise person who has accomplished something significant in life has a concern about those who will control it after he or she is gone. "What will become of this church or this school after I leave?" worries the conscientious pastor or school administrator. "How will my children do with the profitable business that it took me so much energy and knowledge to establish?" wonders the founder of the company. "Will it do harm or good to my son if I leave him 50 million dollars?" reflects the aging financial tycoon.

And those are good questions. After all, the persons who will receive it have not gone through the discipline that at its best builds the strength and character that prepare an individual to manage wisely. Many have been the wrecks in history of children that inherited too much too soon. And it doesn't really have to be all that much. Some people can have their heads turned and be ruined with very little when it comes their way without any work or struggle. While they may or may not be fools, they may not have the slightest idea about how to relate to a windfall in a healthy way.

That is the reason why some very wealthy people in the modern world have set up charitable foundations with boards to manage their accumulated wealth after their death and why some in more modest circumstances have channeled their investments into causes of their own choice before their death. They may love their children too much to just drop everything into their laps. Then again, they may be quite wise in realizing the weaknesses and temptations of those who have never had to exert themselves.

The musings of the Preacher are not unique to him. When he speaks of the injustice of the fool and the wise both getting the same reward; when he sets forth the brutal truth that you can't take it with you, no matter how much you have or how hard you worked for it; when he worries about a fool inheriting his accomplishments; when he thinks such thoughts he represents every older person of wisdom down through the ages.

By the time the Preacher gets to Ecclesiastes 2:23 he has hit the bottom of the bucket. He has demonstrated the meaninglessness of the endless cycle of nature in Ecclesiastes 1:3-11; the meaninglessness of human wisdom in verses 12-18; the meaninglessness of pleasure and wealth in Ecclesiastes 2:1-11; meaninglessness in the face of death in verses 12-17; and the meaninglessness of toil in verses 18-23.

The Preacher has completed his first round of demonstrating his answer to the question at the beginning of his book: "What advantage [profit, lasting benefit] does man have in all his work which he does under the sun?" (1:3). His uniform answer is none. All is absurdity, vanity, meaningless—*hebel*. From an under the sun perspective he has built an airtight case. And he is patiently biding his time before introducing any other viewpoint.

7. Enjoy Life as God Gives It

Ecclesiastes 2:24-26

²⁴There is nothing better for a man than to eat and drink and tell himself that his labor is good. This also I have seen that it is from the hand of God. ²⁵For who can eat and who can have enjoyment without Him? ²⁶For to a person who is good in His sight He has given wisdom and knowledge and joy, while to the sinner He has given the task of gathering and collecting so that he may give to one who is good in God's sight. This too is vanity and striving after wind.

Up to Ecclesiastes 2:24 it has been a pretty depressing book. In fact, it is hard to imagine one more pessimistic. All toil, wisdom, wealth, and pleasure, it declares, is absurd and meaningless.

I want you to consider seriously for a moment all that the Preacher has said and demonstrated in his first two chapters. What would you conclude from such evidence? *That's easy,* you might be thinking, *the obvious conclusion is to argue alongside him that all is vanity. What else can I do, given the fact that he has repeatedly pounded that thesis home?*

Here is where Ecclesiastes' first big surprise surfaces. And it is

> ### A Surprising Conclusion
>
> If the Preacher "were a consistent pessimist, he would urge his readers 'to hate life,' as he . . . does in one passage. His advice would be to escape life, by suicide or by withdrawing from all the idle pleasures of the world" (Jastrow, p. 139).

startling. It just kind of drops out of a clear blue sky without the slightest hint that it is coming. Suddenly after two chapters on meaninglessness we encounter three verses dealing with meaning. But the real shocker is the admonition to find significance and value in some of the things that the Preacher has just finished telling us have no meaning, such as labor and the sensual pleasures of eating and drinking. What are we to make of such an about-face? We will answer that question eventually. But first we need to examine a bit more carefully what he has said.

Please note that throughout the book, as we saw in the outline of Ecclesiastes on pages 25 and 26, the Preacher treats us to repeated demonstrations that life under the sun is only vanity or meaningless. Also note from the outline that he repeatedly drops into the midst of his pessimistic observations what David Hubbard calls an *"alternative conclusion"* (Hubbard, *Ecclesiastes*, p. 92). They are alternatives in the sense that the Preacher has been leading us down the path to one conclusion and then out of nowhere provides us with a second possible interpretation. He does this six times in the book. I am going to quote them in full so that we can get their full force and make comparisons.

1. "There is nothing better for a man than to eat and drink and tell himself that his labor is good. This also I have seen that it is from the hand of God. For who can eat and who can have enjoyment without Him? For to a person who is good in his sight He has given wisdom and knowledge and joy" (2:24-26).

2. "I know that there is nothing better for them than to rejoice and to do good in one's lifetime; moreover, that every man who eats and drinks sees good in all his labor—it is the gift of God" (3:12, 13).

3. "I have seen that nothing is better than that a man should be happy in his activities, for that is his lot. For who will bring him to see what will occur after him?" (3:22).

4. "Here is what I have seen to be good and fitting: to eat, to drink and enjoy oneself in all one's labor in which he toils under the sun during the few years of his life which God has given him; for this is his reward" (5:18).

5. "So I commended pleasure, for there is nothing good for a man under the sun except to eat and to drink and to be merry, and this will stand by him in his toils throughout the days of his life which

God has given him under the sun" (8:15).

6. "Go then, eat your bread in happiness and drink your wine with a cheerful heart; for God has already approved your works. Let your clothes be white all the time, and let not oil be lacking on your head. Enjoy life with the woman whom you love all the days of your fleeting life which He has given to you under the sun; for this is your reward in life and in your toil in which you have labored under the sun. Whatever your hand finds to do, do it with all your might; for there is no activity or planning or knowledge or wisdom in Sheol where you are going" (9:7-10).

By anyone's count that is quite a burst of enjoyment texts for a man who appears most of the time to be an utter pessimist. They have led some scholars to see Ecclesiastes' author as a "preacher of joy" (Whybray, p. xxii). Is he? And if he is, how come he also seems to be an exponent of meaninglessness?

In answering those questions we need to take a closer look at the Preacher's enjoyment passages. The first thing to note is the "there is nothing better" phrases. The exact phrase or its equivalent occurs not only in Ecclesiastes 2:24 but also in 3:12; 3:22; and 8:15. In their contexts the "nothing better than" phrases imply that there is nothing better than what he is recommending *in this short life under the sun*. The Preacher is not giving an absolute, but he is saying that we will find nothing better in the present earthly existence than to eat, drink, and enjoy life.

A second thing that needs to be pointed out is that references to eating and drinking appear in five of the six passages, while toil or work occurs in all six.

Closely coupled with eating, drinking, and laboring in each case is the very definite teaching that such gifts are to be enjoyed. Rejoicing and enjoying in eating, drinking, and toiling is a third major characteristic of the Preacher's alternate conclusions, being mentioned in all six passages.

We can without the slightest doubt conclude that Ecclesiastes is telling us that life as we have it ought to be enjoyed. On the other hand, the Preacher is not saying that enjoyment is the aim of life. To make enjoyment the purpose and goal not only leads to excesses that he does not approve of (see 7:2), but seeking to find the meaning of life in pleasure is the very thing that he ruled as meaningless earlier in Ecclesiastes 2:1-

11. For him such enjoyment is no more than a byproduct in a less than perfect world.

Enjoyment is, furthermore, a gift from God. He emphasizes that fact in five of the six enjoyment passages. Here we have a return to the teaching of Genesis 2:9, in which God pronounces food good. The Preacher agrees with orthodox Judaism, which taught that a gracious God is the giver of every gift, and that we ought to enjoy them with thanksgiving. It is not a call to hedonism but rather an uplifting of the teaching that God made His children able to find pleasure in the good things of life.

A fifth theme running through the six enjoyment passages is the reality of human limits. Three of the passages utilize an "under the sun" frame of reference, and five of them hint at death and/or the temporariness of life. As Derek Kidner, observes, "these joys, however innocent, are passing, like all else that is 'under the sun'" (Kidner, *Wisdom,* p. 100).

With the reality of the threat of death and humanity's earthly limitations always lurking in the shadows, we find the Preacher putting his encouragement to enjoy earthly pleasures in their proper context. Enjoying life may be "better than" utter futility, but it too will come to an end. While enjoying life may be our "reward" (see 5:18; 9:9) during our earthly existence, the Preacher never equates it with ultimate profit. In the end the grave takes each of us and the pleasure stops. Thus he can even speak of vanity or meaninglessness in the context of God's good gifts (2:26). In fact, that is his conclusion to his first enjoyment passage. In effect, he is saying, "Enjoy the good gifts of God while you can, but it will soon be over. Then you will once again face the absurdity of death."

In conclusion, Ecclesiastes' six enjoyment passages are important, but we must read them within the context of the entire book. One important lesson we learn is that in this earthly life we should not expect anything better than the simple pleasures that we can glean from daily life. If we don't try to make this life meet *all* our needs we will find that "there is nothing better" than God's gifts that lead to enjoyment during our earthbound existence. We must avoid all false optimism regarding life's possibilities. Kidner points out that what spoils our daily enjoyments "is our hunger to get out of them more than they can give" (Kidner, *Message,* p. 35). They may be good in themselves but they are not the answer to life's meaning. As Tremper Longman notes, "if there is no ultimate meaning in wisdom or one's work, then one must look to enjoy life as the opportunities present themselves" (Longman, p. 106). Such is the good advice of the Preacher.

The good news is that God gives "wisdom and knowledge" as well as "joy" to those who seek to do His will (Eccl. 2:26). The first two of those gifts should help the one "who is good in His sight" to put life's experiences in proper perspective. But those who reject God's will (the sinners of 2:26) will continue to flounder as they fruitlessly strive for meaning and purpose, all the while looking in the wrong place. And that too is "vanity and striving after wind" (verse 26).

In the enjoyment passage of Ecclesiastes 2:24-26 we have what Michael Eaton calls the "antithesis of secular pessimism." "The Preacher," he writes, "has held before his readers two ways of life: the vicious circle of a pointless world, temporary pleasures, fruitless work, futile wisdom, inevitable death, versus an enjoyable life taken daily from the hand of God, in the 'assurance of faith' that he deals appropriately with [the] righteous and [the] unrighteous" (Eaton, pp. 76, 77).

8. The Uselessness of Striving Against the Rounds of Nature

Ecclesiastes 3:1-22

[1]*There is an appointed time for everything. And there is a time for every event under heaven—*

[2]*A time to give birth*
     and a time to die;
A time to plant
     and a time to uproot
     what is planted.
[3]*A time to kill*
     and a time to heal;
A time to tear down
     and a time to build up.
[4]*A time to weep*
     and a time to laugh;
A time to mourn
     and a time to dance.
[5]*A time to throw stones*
     and a time to gather stones;
A time to embrace
     and a time to shun embracing.
[6]*A time to search*
     and a time to give up as lost;
A time to keep
     and a time to throw away.
[7]*A time to tear apart*
     and a time to sew together;

A time to be silent
> *and a time to speak.*
[8]*A time to love*
> *and a time to hate;*
A time for war
> *and a time for peace.*
[9]*What profit is there to the worker from that in which he toils?* [10]*I have seen the task which God has given the sons of men with which to occupy themselves.* [11]*He has made everything appropriate in its time. He has also set eternity in their heart, yet so that man will not find out the work which God has done from the beginning even to the end.*

[12]*I know that there is nothing better for them than to rejoice and to do good in one's lifetime;* [13]*moreover, that every man who eats and drinks sees good in all his labor—it is the gift of God.* [14]*I know that everything God does will remain forever; there is nothing to add to it and there is nothing to take from it, for God has so worked that men should fear Him.* [15]*That which is has been already and that which will be has already been, for God seeks what has passed by.*

[16]*Furthermore, I have seen under the sun that in the place of justice there is wickedness and in the place of righteousness there is wickedness.* [17]*I said to myself, "God will judge both the righteous man and the wicked man," for a time for every matter and for every deed is there.* [18]*I said to myself concerning the sons of men, "God has surely tested them in order for them to see that they are but beasts."* [19]*For the fate of the sons of men and the fate of beasts is the same. As one dies so dies the other; indeed, they all have the same breath [spirit] and there is no advantage for man over beast, for all is vanity.* [20]*All go to the same place. All came from the dust and all return to the dust.* [21]*Who knows that the breath [spirit] of man ascends upward and the breath [spirit] of the beast descends downward to the earth?* [22]*I have seen that nothing is better than that man should be happy in his activities, for that is his lot. For who will bring him to see what will occur after him?*

There is a time for everything. That's good. Just think of the terrible confusion if the time to plant sometimes fell in June but in other years in December or October. Our passage lets us know in no uncertain terms that God is in control of the affairs of this earth (3:11, 14, 15). The regularity and faithfulness of the laws of nature make human existence both livable and to a certain extent predictable.

That is the good side of the fact that there is "an appointed time for everything" (3:1). But it is certainly not the only aspect. The major emphasis of Ecclesiastes 3 is the oppressiveness of time sequences that humans can neither alter (verse 14, 15) nor fully understand (verse 11). As Roland Murphy observes, the Preacher offers "this poem on time in order to underscore the sad human condition. These are *God's* times, not our times. They happen to us; they are under divine control" (Murphy, *Ecclesiastes,* p. 39).

The poem itself consists of 14 pairs of contrasts. Its breadth of coverage implies that all human activities are caught up in the unceasing flow of fixed times.

We find ourselves reminded of the cycles of nature poem in the first chapter (verses 4-11) as we read the time poem of chapter 3. But there is an extremely important difference. In Ecclesiastes 1 the Preacher uses the ceaseless activity of such impersonal things as blowing wind and flowing rivers, but here he deals with events that involve human activity. It is at least understandable that we can't control or fully understand the forces of nature, but what about those things of the human realm?

The Message rendering of Ecclesiastes 3:9-11 captures the frustration of the Preacher in the face of the tyranny of time: "But in the end, does it really make a difference what anyone does? I've had a good look at what God has given us to do—busywork, mostly. True, God made everything beautiful in itself and in its time—but he's left us in the dark, so we can never know what God is up to, whether he's coming or going."

Before leaving verses 9-11 we need to examine one item a bit more closely. Verse 11 very plainly states that God has placed "eternity" in the human heart or mind. Here we have an aspect of life that differentiates humans from animals. Humans have a concern with both meaning and time in its past and future aspects. It is a part of our nature that we can't escape from. Walter Kaiser suggests that the human quest for overall meaning "is a deep-seated desire, a compulsive drive, because man is made in the image of God to appreciate the beauty of creation . . . ; to know the character, composition, and meaning of the world . . . ; and to discern its purpose and destiny" (Kaiser, p. 66). But the sad news from the Preacher's under the sun perspective is that no matter how hard we try, we can't really understand. In terms of time, we can fit into its flow but because of who we are we can never hope to control it. Here again we come face to face with the meaninglessness of life and human toil (1:3).

In such frustrating circumstances, he advises, "there is nothing better for [people] than to rejoice and to do good in one's lifetime" (3:12). That is, humanity's best option in its present frustrating existence is to enjoy the good gifts of God in eating, and drinking, and, working (verse 13). "To do good" in such a situation is to "do the best we can while we are still alive" (verse 12, TEV). As usual, the pall of death is never far from the Preacher's thinking. Tremper Longman suggests that it is important to note that Ecclesiastes' counsel in verses 12 and 13 "is not the highest, best imaginable good but life in a fallen world, which is the best humans can do under the circumstances" (Longman, p. 122).

Ecclesiastes 3:14 and 15 take us back to the time emphasis of the poem in verses 1-8. Their basic thrust is that we might as well submit to God's will since we can't change the shape of reality or the unstoppable flow of time. In short, the paragraph running from verses 12-15 tells us that rather than beating our heads against brick walls we need to accept things as they are and enjoy the present life to the best of our ability.

But the Preacher doesn't seem to be very good at following his own advice. In verse 16 he again begins struggling with meaninglessness and absurdity. In the places of righteousness and justice he found wickedness. What could be more absurd than encountering wickedness in the very places that are supposed to be eradicating the problem?

That preposterous situation brings the Preacher back to the concept of time. Since everything has a time there must be a time for God to execute judgment for both the righteous and the wicked (verse 17). Implied in the sequence of verses is the idea that "the changing of the times (cf. 3:1-8)" has not only allowed "wickedness but also limits its duration. In this way the changing of the times also implements something like a 'divine judgment'" (Krüger, p. 91). In Jewish thinking the concept of judgment not only suggests a "judicial assessment but the execution of sentence also" (Eaton, p. 84). The Preacher doesn't explain what he means by judgment or seek to locate it in time, but for him events call for one and he has no doubt that it will happen. The thought that the God who rules over everything will eventually put things right comforts the Preacher, at least temporarily.

But the feeling doesn't last very long. Verse 18 finds him pondering the fact that humans have not lived up to their possibilities. Their actions, as he noted in verse 16, have certainly all too often proven to be beastly.

God may have created humans in His image (Gen. 1:26, 27), but from an under the sun perspective they resemble more what evolutionary biologist Desmond Morris labels "The Naked Ape." Picking up on that title, some have observed that humans living an under the sun existence are too often "an insult to the ape family" (Davidson, p. 26).

Be that as it may, the Preacher is soon back to one of his favorite negative topics—death. His thoughts about people being no better than beasts leads him to compare the death of humans to that of animals. All, including the rulings of the judgment in verse 17, is meaningless, he cries out in verse 19, because humans are finite. They like the animals are subject to death. Both humans and animals "go to the same place. All came from the dust and all return to the dust. Who knows that the breath [spirit] of man ascends upward and the breath [spirit] of the beast descends downward" (verses 20, 21).

In that picture of death we find the Preacher going back to the creation of humanity in Genesis 2:7. There we read that "God formed man of dust from the ground, and breathed into his nostrils the breath of life; and man became a living being." Ecclesiastes 3:20, 21 sees death as the reverse of the creation process, with the body returning to dust (cf. Gen. 3:19) as breathing ceases. Humans may have been created in the image of God, but from the Preacher's under the sun perspective they die like animals. From strictly empirical observation no one can prove that humans have a heavenly destiny. These under the sun verses offer no hint of an afterlife. So much for human dignity and meaning. Once again the Preacher concludes that "all is vanity," meaninglessness (Eccl. 3:19).

What to do in such a situation? You know his answer by now. From an under the sun viewpoint there can be nothing "better than that man should be happy in his activities, for that is his lot" or God's gift (verse 22, 13). He concludes the chapter with the thought that people do not know what will come after them (verse 22).

The Preacher offers us more than a bit of wisdom when he suggests that we shouldn't fret forever over those things we can't know or control but should get on with enjoying the little things of daily life. Jesus offered similar counsel in his teaching on worry in the Sermon on the Mount (Matt. 6:25-34). But Jesus didn't stop there. He and His apostles made the nature of the future life abundantly clear. The New Testament from its above the sun perspective offers Christians hope in both the judgment and the promised kingdom. There will come an end to the ceaseless seasons of time when "the kingdom of the world has become the kingdom of our Lord and of his Christ; and He will reign forever and ever" (Rev. 11:15).

9. The Uselessness of Striving in an Unjust World

Ecclesiastes 4:1–16

¹Then I looked again at all the acts of oppression which were being done under the sun. And behold I saw the tears of the oppressed and that they had no one to comfort them; and on the side of their oppressors was power, but they had no one to comfort them. ²So I congratulated the dead who are already dead more than the living who are still living. ³But better off than both of them is the one who has never existed, who has never seen the evil activity that is done under the sun.

⁴I have seen that every labor and every skill which is done is the result of rivalry between a man and his neighbor. This too is vanity and striving after wind. ⁵The fool folds his hands and consumes his own flesh. ⁶One hand full of rest is better than two fists full of labor and striving after wind.

⁷Then I looked again at vanity under the sun. ⁸There was a certain man without a dependent, having neither a son nor a brother, yet there was no end to all his labor. Indeed, his eyes were not satisfied with riches and he never asked, "And for whom am I laboring and depriving myself of pleasure?" This too is vanity and it is a grievous task.

⁹Two are better than one because they have a good return for their labor. ¹⁰For if either of them falls, the one will lift up his companion. But woe to the one who falls when there is not another to lift him up. ¹¹Furthermore, if two lie down together they keep warm, but how can one be warm alone? ¹²And if one can overpower him who is alone, two can resist him. A cord of three strands is not quickly torn apart.

¹³A poor yet wise lad is better than an old and foolish king who no longer knows how to receive instruction. ¹⁴For he has come out of prison to become king, even though he was born poor in his kingdom. ¹⁵I have seen all the living under the sun throng to the side of the second lad who replaces him. ¹⁶There is no end to all the people, to all who were before them, and even the ones who will come later will not be happy with him, for this too is vanity and striving after wind.

Up through the end of chapter 3 Ecclesiastes has set forth a progressive argument that runs fairly smoothly from one point to the next. Beginning with the fourth chapter the Preacher's book takes on more of the texture of the book of Proverbs. But even then it is not mere proverbs, but proverbial sayings mixed in with the personal experience observations that characterized the book's opening chapters. The argument in chapters 4-10, therefore, is not as easily outlined as those that precede and follow them.

Nevertheless, the proverbial sayings and personal insights of those chapters cluster around specific themes. A major one running through the five paragraphs of Ecclesiastes 4 involves the uselessness or futility of striving in an unjust world.

The Preacher begins his fourth chapter (verses 1-3) with a dismal picture of oppression. Yet, while the mistreatment of the weak deeply troubles him, he calls for no social reform such as we find in the prophets (see, e.g., Amos 5:21-24, Micah 6:8). He appears to accept oppression as a sad fact of life, but one that seriously disturbs him, as seen by his threefold use of "oppression," "oppressed," and "oppressor" in one verse.

> ## The Progression of Chapter 4
>
> 1. The uselessness of striving against oppression (verses 1-3).
> 2. The uselessness of competitive striving (verses 4-6).
> 3. The uselessness of striving as an end in itself (verses 7, 8).
> 4. The uselessness of striving alone (verses 9-12).
> 5. The uselessness of striving for fame (verses 13-16).

Most concerned with the oppressed, he notes their tears, but, Michael Fox asserts, "what troubles Qohelet in these tears is less the misery the tears express than the absence of a humane response to the suffering. This emphasis is shown by the repetition of the clause 'and they have no comforter'" (Fox, *A Time to Tear Down*, p. 218). While he does not much expect the oppression to disappear or its victims to stop weeping, he is upset to the depth of his soul that no one seems to care. His theme of the strength that comes from mutual caring and sympathy he will reinforce in verses 9-12, in which he asserts the need to support others in their journey through life.

The Preacher is also concerned with the power of the oppressor. Gone from Israel were the safeguards of the Mosaic law that stipulated that the rich must look out for the poor and seek to make their lives livable (see, e.g., Deut. 24:17-22). Of course, as Derek Kidner indicates, the Preacher undoubtedly recognized "that there is no coincidence in the fact that power is found on the side of the oppressor, since it is power that most quickly breeds the habit of oppression" (Kidner, *Message,* p. 44). Lord Acton put it a bit differently when he penned that "power corrupts and absolute power tends to corrupt absolutely."

The misuse of power and the lack of concern for the oppressed brought the Preacher to absolute despair. He had come to the place where he concluded that

1. Death is better than life (verse 2).
2. But better still is never having been born to witness such a world (verse 3).

We find no striving here—only total depression. Our dysfunctional world is too messed up even to live in. His desire is to escape into nothingness. At this time in his experience he would agree with seventeenth-century philosopher Thomas Hobbes, who wrote that human life is "solitary, poore, nasty, brutish, and short" (*Leviathan,* part 1, chapter 13). But, we must note, such despair appears to be a question of mood with the Preacher. In other places he is quite certain that it is better to be "a live dog than a dead lion" (9:4). His depressed thinking, like ours, is not always logically consistent.

Chapter 4's second paragraph (verses 4-6) takes us to the depths of human motivation. Why is it that those of us who overwork spend our lives that way? Oh, we have a ready answer: We are caring for our families, contributing to society, enjoy work more than anything else, and so on. Here the Preacher violently disagrees with us, claiming that the basic motivation for our striving is rivalry. We want to be better than the next person, desire the top spot, and crave recognition that we are the best (verse 4).

All of us have some of that spirit in us. And its not totally bad. We should strive to make the best contribution we can. But when we feel crushed when someone else achieves more than us or gets more recognition it is time to sit still and think about why we are doing what we do.

Striving against the competition as an end in itself is a sickness rather than a virtue. In the words of the Preacher, it is meaningless (verse 4). He then cites two proverbs. On the one hand, he notes that persons who do nothing not only cannot feed their families but they cannibalize their sense of worth (verse 5). The second proverb uplifts the wisdom of enjoying "one hand full of rest" over "two fists full of labor" that has no reward but the work itself (verse 6). Both proverbs are true. They point to the need for moderation even in striving in the workplace.

The third paragraph in chapter 4 treats the uselessness of striving as an end in itself (verses 7, 8). Here we find those individuals who keep pushing for more long after they have already cared for all of their needs. Their aim in life is to accumulate wealth, even though they don't even have anyone to leave it to.

Two things especially stand out in the behavior of the man the Preacher describes in verses 8. First, the external aspect: he never ceases laboring ("there was no end to all his labor"). Second, the internal: he never feels satisfied with what he has. Yet he is depriving himself of a meaningful existence and making his life "grievous." In the end he never sits down and asks himself why he strives as he does. Such an existence, the Preacher exclaims, is meaningless.

Chapter 4's fourth paragraph ties in with thoughts in the previous two and sets forth the uselessness of striving alone (verses 9-12). Ernest Hengstenberg nicely summarizes the central core of the first 12 verses of the chapter when he writes, "How little the life of a man depends on many possessions, the author shows in a picturesque description of the example of a rich man who has so completely isolated himself by his selfishness and avarice, that he stands alone and deserted, without enjoyment and without protection in life" (Hengstenberg, p. 128).

Verses 9-12 with their teaching that "two are better than one" is one of the most widely cited passages in Ecclesiastes. People have used the passage in everything from marriage sermons to labor negotiations. But no matter how others may have used or misused it, its central teaching is both important and true. That is, "one of God's great gifts in helping us deal with problems of oppression, poverty, loneliness, and injustice is the company of others" (Hubbard, *Beyond Futility*, p. 62).

Whether we stumble and need someone to help us up, are sleeping and want someone to keep us warm, or are being attacked and require the protection of numbers, "two are better than one" (verse 9) and the strength of three is better yet (verse 12). Striving in endless competition with others is not only vanity (verse 4), it is not optimally productive. Why senselessly struggle to do it on our own, says the Preacher, when we can do it better in the companionship of others.

The last paragraph deals with the meaninglessness of striving after fame in an ever changing world (verses 13-16). Ecclesiastes illustrates the foolishness of it all in a two stage parable. In the rags to riches stage a wise young nothing of a person succeeds an old fool of a king who no longer took advise. He is truly a success, and he is undoubtedly popular in the eyes of the people. Yet another young man eventually replaces him, and "all the living under the sun throng" to the new hero's side (verse 15) just as they had to his predecessor's. The replacement-of-hero syndrome, the Preacher observes, has no end. And in the long run people will ultimately find fault with every new hero. Racing after popularity and fame, he concludes, is nothing less than wind chasing and vanity (verse 16).

Ecclesiastes 4 is a chapter that we all need to ponder. Why, we must ask ourselves, are we doing what we do? Are we capitalizing on even the limited meaning that we can have in our under the sun earthly life or are we endlessly striving for those things that are transient, unsatisfying, or even evil? Chapter 4 is a call to vital introspection. There is a good chance that the Preacher may be speaking to us personally in one or more of the five teachings of Ecclesiastes 4. It is time to wake up to ourselves and our motivations.

10. Advice on Religious Topics

Ecclesiastes 5:1-7

¹Guard your steps as you go to the house of God and draw near to listen rather than to offer the sacrifice of fools; for they do not know they are doing evil. ²Do not be hasty in word or impulsive in thought to bring up a matter in the presence of God. For God is in heaven and you are on the earth; therefore let your words be few. ³For the dream comes through much effort and the voice of a fool through many words.

⁴When you make a vow to God, do not be late in paying it; for He takes no delight in fools. Pay what you vow! ⁵It is better that you should not vow than that you should vow and not pay. ⁶Do not let your speech cause you to sin and do not say in the presence of the messenger of God that it was a mistake. Why should God be angry on account of your voice and destroy the work of your hands?

⁷For in many dreams and in many words there is emptiness. Rather, fear God.

Ecclesiastes' theme is clear enough! All is vanity or meaninglessness under the sun and in all of our work we find no real gain or profit (1:2, 3). The Preacher has pounded that theme home in two mighty demonstrations, the first running from Ecclesiastes 1:4-2:26 and the second going from 3:1-4:16.

In chapter 5 he moves from his theme that everything under the sun—all human wisdom and toil and even the cycles of nature—is absurd to providing his readers with some words of advice. The first seven verses speak to religion while verses 8-20 focus on more earthly or secular topics. But even tucked into his words on worship he manages to highlight unhealthy practices that make worship itself meaningless, vain, absurd, and fruitless. It is true that he offers some sound advice on how to worship God but he sets that positive advice against a backdrop of those who manage to be "fools" even in their relationship to God. The Preacher treats worship in terms of sacrifice, prayer, and vows, but doing any or all of them as a fool is a common thread that runs through his discussion. It is one of the sad facts of life that human beings can take even the best of things and pervert them.

Before examining the implications of Ecclesiastes 5:1-7, perhaps we should stand back and take a look at the characteristics of the Preacher's advice sections, which form major portions of his book (4:9-12; 5:1-12; 7:1-8:9; 9:13-12:7). For one thing, they tend to emphasize proverbial sayings. Some of the Preacher's proverbs are admonitions telling people what to do. Others are sayings describing how life works, often implying the proper way to behave. And still others are proverbs of comparison, often beginning with the word "better." His comparative proverbs highlight the advantage of one form of conduct over another (see La Sor, p. 594).

> Ecclesiastes 5:1-7 leaves us with the distinct impression that the Preacher is much more in harmony with Old Testament piety than we may have surmised from his first four chapters.

A second characteristic of the advice sections is that, in common with the book of Proverbs in the Old Testament and the letter of James in the New, the subjects under discussion change more frequently than in those sections of Ecclesiastes that focus on demonstrating the vanity of life's under the sun activities and aspirations. A third characteristic is that the Preacher uses the term "vanity" less frequently.

Moving to Ecclesiastes 5:1, we come to a section that demonstrates that our author is not the agnostic or atheist that he may have sounded like in his first four chapters. The Preacher demonstrates that he not only has an interest in God but that he is extremely perceptive on the true meaning of worship, more so than many priests and other religious leaders whom we find in the pages of the Bible. These verses give us more than a hint that the Preacher is much closer to Old Testament piety than we may have thought thus far in his book.

"Guard your steps as you go to the house of God and draw near to listen rather than to offer the sacrifice of fools," the Preacher tells us in strident tones (5:1). Reflecting upon this verse, Alexander MacLaren points out the crucial truth that "fruitful and acceptable worship begins before it begins" (MacLaren, p. 351).

Significantly, the Preacher launches his treatment of worship before the worshipper even gets to the house of God. Expounding upon that thought MacLaren notes that a fruitful worship service starts at least the night before as people prepare their hearts to hear God's word for them. As MacLaren puts it, "what likelihood is there that much good will come of worship to people who talk politics or scandal right up to the church door? Is reading newspapers in the pews . . . a good preparation for worshipping God? The heaviest rain runs off parched ground, unless it has been first softened by a gentle fall of moisture. Hearts that have no dew of previous meditation to make them receptive are not likely to drink in much of the showers of blessing which may be falling round them" (*ibid.*, p. 352).

He has a good point. A Sabbath morning blessing, no matter how good it is, is always better if the heart and mind has been in a state of preparation since Sabbath eve. It is probably no accident that the Jewish Sabbath began at sunset on Friday evening. That gave believers time to guard their steps as they moved toward the house of God (Eccl. 5:1).

Of course, not all worshippers understand. The Preacher makes that clear in the second half of verse 1, in which he speaks of the "sacrifice of fools." The foolish sacrifice results from those who have not drawn "near to listen." As a consequence, they really don't understand what they are doing. Those who go through the ritual but miss its meaning offer "the sacrifice of fools." It is the opposite of the understanding of David, who wrote:

> "For You do not delight in sacrifice,
>   otherwise I would give it;
> You are not pleased with burnt offering.
> The sacrifices of God are a broken spirit;
> A broken and a contrite heart, O God,
>   You will not despise" (Ps. 51:16, 17).

"To listen" (Eccl. 5:1) from the perspective of the Hebrew mindset meant not only to hear but to obey. Samuel reflected that understanding when he said to Saul, who had just offered "the sacrifice of fools,"

> "Has the Lord as much delight in burnt
>   offerings and sacrifices
> As in obeying the voice of the Lord?
> Behold, to obey is better than sacrifice,
> And to heed than the fat of rams" (1 Sam. 15:22).

Jesus also spoke to the point when He claimed that "not every one who says to me, 'Lord, Lord,' shall enter the kingdom of heaven, but he who does the will of my Father" (Matt. 7:21, RSV).

Down through history, unfortunately, there have been more than enough religious fools to go around. They not only offer meaningless sacrifices but they babble along in what they think is a prayer to God. What Ecclesiastes 5:2, 3 finds fault with is prayer in which people do not know whom they are talking to or what they are mumbling about. But whatever they lack in understanding they make up for by the repetition of words and phrases. The sad fact, the Preacher points out, is that we can even be fools in our prayers. "What is condemned," MacLaren asserts, "is words which travel faster than thoughts or feelings, or which proceed from hearts that have not been brought into patient submission, or from such as lack reverent realization of God's majesty" (MacLaren, p. 353).

Once again, Jesus reflected on meaningless repetitive prayers in the Sermon on the Mount (Matt. 6:7). The prayer of the non-fool is one in which the worshipper has listened to God (Eccl. 5:1), respects who He is (verse 2), and has thought through both the meaning of prayer and what he or she is praying about. But how many prayers, as verse 3 indicates, are like "unsubstantial" dreams. They are just "so many words [that] produce foolish and empty prayer" (J. S. Wright, p. 1168).

The Preacher's third illustration of foolish worship deals with those who have made vows to God and then have no hurry or no desire to pay what they have promised Him (Eccl. 5:4-6). They apparently had no difficulty remembering that He was in heaven while they were on a troubled earth (verse 2) when they had a problem they wanted Him to solve or when they needed rescuing from disaster. But after promising Him almost anything for help they forget about both their promise and who He is after things get better.

God does not take such carelessness lightly—"He takes no delight in fools" (verse 4). It is better, the Preacher comments, not to vow at all than not to pay or to claim that you made a mistake in offering the promise. The implications for those who do so, according to verse 6, is that God will conclude that He made a mistake in rescuing such a fool. The moral of the story is that we should not "play religious games" with God (Longman, p. 154).

But oh how hard it is not to play games when we find ourselves in a tight spot. Of course we are sincere when the pressure is on. We only forget when things improve.

Verse 7 sets forth the alternative to being a religious fool: "Fear God." Those who fear Him will be fully aware of who He is (that He is in heaven while they are on earth, verse 2), will guard their steps as they approach His worship (verse 1), and will "listen" with both ears to all that He has to say (verse 1). Such individuals will find meaningful rather than meaningless worship because they "fear God" and have a relationship with Him.

> "This writer's target is the well-meaning person who likes a good sing and turns up cheerfully enough to church; but who listens with half an ear, and never quite gets round to what he has volunteered to do for God. . . . Such a man has forgotten where and who he is; above all, who God is" (Kidner, *Message*, pp. 52, 53).

Before leaving the "fear God" of Ecclesiastes 5:7, we should note that some students of the book see those words to be the theological center of the book (see Dorsey, pp. 198, 195, 197). The fact that Ecclesiastes closes with that same command (12:13) supports such an interpretation. To fear Him does not so much mean to be afraid of God as it does to respect, love, and obey Him because of who we are and who He is. It is the fear of God, the Preacher tells us, that makes the difference between foolish and meaningful worship. No greater tragedy can happen than for worship to become just one more meaningless under the sun activity.

11. The Futility of Riches

Ecclesiastes 5:8-20

⁸*If you see oppression of the poor and denial of justice and righteousness in the province, do not be shocked at the sight; for one official watches over another official, and there are higher officials over them.* ⁹*After all, a king who cultivates the field is an advantage to the land.*

¹⁰*He who loves money will not be satisfied with money, nor he who loves abundance with its income. This too is vanity.* ¹¹*When good things increase, those who consume them increase. So what is the advantage to their owners except to look on?* ¹²*The sleep of the working man is pleasant, whether he eats little or much; but the full stomach of the rich man does not allow him to sleep.*

¹³*There is a grievous evil which I have seen under the sun: riches being hoarded by their owner to his hurt.* ¹⁴*When those riches were lost through a bad investment and he had fathered a son, then there was nothing to support him.* ¹⁵*As he had come naked from his mother's womb, so will he return as he came. He will take nothing from the fruit of his labor that he can carry in his hand.* ¹⁶*This also is a grievous evil—exactly as a man is born, thus will he die. So what is the advantage to him who toils for the wind?* ¹⁷*Throughout his life he also eats in darkness with great vexation, sickness and anger.*

¹⁸*Here is what I have seen to be good and fitting: to eat, to drink and enjoy oneself in all one's labors in which he toils under the sun during the few years of his life which God has given him; for this is his reward.* ¹⁹*Furthermore, as for every man to whom God has given riches and wealth, He has also empowered him to eat from them and to receive his reward and rejoice in his labor; this is the gift of God.* ²⁰*For he will not often consider the years of his life, because God keeps him occupied with the gladness of his heart.*

The Futility of Riches

Whereas Ecclesiastes 5:1-7 offered insights on religion, Ecclesiastes 5:8-6:12 centers on worldly issues, providing advice on them (5:8-12) and a demonstration of the futility of wealth (5:13-6:12).

With Ecclesiastes 5:8, 9 we are back to a familiar topic—oppression, a subject the Preacher raised earlier in 3:16 and 4:1-3. While he has treated oppression previously, this is the first time he has brought in the role of government in injustice. But the line of argument is quite in harmony with the discussion in chapter 3, in which the Preacher noted that "in the place of justice there is wickedness" (verse 16), and in chapter 4, in which he pointed out that no one comforts the poor and oppressed at the bottom of the social heap (verse 1). It certainly couldn't be governmental officials if they are the ones doing the afflicting.

That seems to be the teaching of Ecclesiastes 5:8, which has "people of rank" watching over, or looking out for, "their subordinates, making it impossible to protect against corruption" (Fox, *A Time to Tear Down*, p. 234). Thus we find oppression of the poor because of the officials, not in spite of them. From top to bottom the authorities watch out or cover up for one another.

Unlike the prophets, who cry out for justice in such situations (Isa. 1:10-17; Micah 6:6-8), the Preacher merely says that we should not be shocked (5:8). Or as one author puts it, "Koheleth is no revolutionary. . . . He seems to regard a bureaucratic government as a necessary evil, even if it inevitably means that some get rich at the expense of others" (Davis, p. 196).

But, we need to ask in the face of verse 9, how does the king fit into the picture? The context suggests that this verse continues the thought of the previous one. Thus the "line of corruption goes to the very top; *even the king* himself takes advantage of his politically powerful position to get the *profit of the land*" (Longman, p. 158).

While that interpretation might not agree with the New American Standard Bible translation given above, it harmonizes with the obscure Hebrew of verse 9. The New International Version renders the text as "the increase from the land is taken by all; the king himself profits from the fields." At any rate, it appears that corruption and oppression exists from the top to the bottom of the government. That condition, of course, has been a problem across history. Fallen humans in their selfishness all too easily become oppressors of those weaker than themselves.

Ecclesiastes 5:10-12 shifts from governmental greed to greed in general. The passage consists of a chain of proverbs, with the one in verse 10 stating the thesis that money doesn't satisfy and the next two verses supplying additional illustrations of the main point. We may summarize the overall teaching of the passage with the thought that "if anything is worse than the addiction money brings, it is the emptiness it leaves" (Kidner, *Message*, p. 56).

The Preacher raises the issue of the "love" of money in verse 10, a text that reminds us of Paul's saying that "the love of money is the root of all evils" (1 Tim. 6:10, RSV). Ecclesiastes doesn't go that far, but it does emphasize its frustrating qualities, not the least of which is that no matter how

Reasons Why the Pursuit of Wealth Is Not a Satisfying Life Goal

1. "Wealth is both addictive and unsatisfactory" (verse 10).
2. "Wealth attracts human leeches" (verse 11).
3. "Wealth does not give peace or rest" (verse 12).
4. "Love of wealth often causes a person to hoard even to the point causing suffering to himself" (verse 13).
5. "Wealth is an insecure basis for happiness since it may be easily lost in a bad business venture" (verse 14).
6. "Wealth is certain to disappear at death" (verse 15).
   —Garrett, p. 314

much money those who love it may have they always want more. The Bible teaches that some loves are healthy and wholesome (such as the love of God or one's family), but that the love of money is a meaningless enterprise. Money has its uses, but when it becomes an end in itself we end up lost and frustrated.

Verse 11 raises the problem that when individuals get wealth they also acquire a flock of new "friends." Such individuals may be sponging family members, necessary employees, or both. Many are the famous persons who found unlimited admirers and hangers-on in their heyday, only to be left to an obscure and lonely end when their funds ran out. George Barton nicely sums up the final part of verse 11 when he writes that "one can really enjoy but a limited amount of wealth, he who has more, has only the pleasure of seeing others consume it" (Barton, p. 127).

Ecclesiastes 5:12 raises the fact that the rich don't sleep as well as working people. Some may eat too much for good rest, while others may suffer from increased anxiety over protecting what they have and/or their addictive desire to get more, but the result is the same—insomnia and perhaps ill health related to the tensions of a stressful life.

Verses 13-17 provide a thumbnail sketch of a man toiling and hoarding his money, harming himself in the process through self-deprivation and excess worry, only to lose it all at one swoop in a bad investment. He fathers a son, but has nothing either to support him with or to leave him as an inheritance. Eventually he exits the world with nothing. It is the story of a man who ruined his life twice over—once in acquiring wealth and a second time in losing it. Truly, says the Preacher, his love of wealth was "a grievous evil," vain, and meaningless—a chasing of wind and a demonstration of his thesis in Ecclesiastes 1:3 that there is no advantage or lasting benefit to all one's toil under the sun. And, as usual with the Preacher, if anyone thinks they have any advantage, in the end the ubiquitous death that faces every person under the sun will gobble it up.

> ## The Paradox of Wealth
>
> "It is one of the ironies of life today in our affluent Western society that having eliminated many of the crippling diseases associated with poverty, our killer diseases are now the diseases of affluence: coronary attacks, lung cancer, liver failure. We over-indulge and then spend millions on diet control and low calorie foods. We purchase exercise machines to tone up the body we have been neglecting and undermining" (Davidson, p. 39).

The passage is closely related to verses 10-12, which present the rich person who toils in discomfort. But at least the person in verse 12 got to eat to the full. This one doesn't even enjoy his food. "Throughout his life he also eats in darkness with great vexation, sickness and anger" (verse 17). His concern with wealth blocked him from even the simplest forms of human pleasure.

The totality of his focus has been on getting. And then what he has acquired is gone. As a result, no one gets any enjoyment—not even his heir. Ecclesiastes 5:14 is not the first time the Preacher has dealt with heirs. In 2:19 he expressed frustration about the possibility of the heir being a fool. But in 4:8 things get worse, with the Preacher brooding over the thought of a worker having no heir to leave hard earned wealth to. But in 5:14 the worker has a son but has nothing to leave him. In a world in which survival depended upon preserving family resources, this truly was a disaster.

Verses 18-20 are a direct take off of verse 17, which pictures the miser miserably eating in darkness and distress. Here is a person who hasn't yet seen the foolishness of an acquisitive lifestyle that in reality is no better than chasing the wind (verse 16).

In verse 18 the Preacher offers a deliberate contrast to the fool's life of verse 17. Once again, in the face of the futility of chasing material wealth and the absolute certainty of death, the biblical author claims the best thing that we can do is to enjoy the life that God has given us during our short earthly existence. That modest pleasure is the "reward" God makes available on earth for those able and willing to see the rat race of acquiring more and more for what it is.

Ecclesiastes 5:18-20 is the fourth occurrence of the advice to enjoy life thus far (see section 7 for a discussion of this theme). The key word in these verses is "God," mentioned four times in three verses.

- It is God who gives us life (verse 18).
- It is God who gives riches (verse 19).
- It is God who gives us the ability to enjoy food and life's other simple pleasures (verse 19).
- It is God who gives us gladness of heart (verse 20).

Getting back to the message of Genesis, the Preacher has no doubt that God made the world good and that He created it for human enjoyment (Gen. 1, 2) in spite of the Fall and the under the sun conditions that have existed since that time (see Gen. 3, especially verses 17-19).

In closing, we should remember that God is not against wealth. Some of the great heroes of Scripture were wealthy, including Abraham, Jacob, Joseph, and Daniel. The problem, as the Preacher has pointed out, is the all-consuming "love" of wealth, which in itself is a form of idolatry since it thrusts itself into our line of priorities before God.

Here we have a temptation that faces us all. The worship of wealth is not a rich person's sport. We can all participate. After all, the poor are just as focused on getting a few extra pennies or rags as the rich are in raking in their millions. Apparently the tendency to put wealth first in our life came with sin itself. Whether we like it or not we are all a part of the problem. That means you my friend. It even includes me.

Jesus reads our hearts. His message to each of us is the same: "Do not lay up for yourselves treasures on earth, . . . but lay up for yourselves treasures in heaven . . . . For where your treasure is, there will your heart be also" (Matt. 6:19-21, RSV). Not bad advice for those of us who desire to avoid being wind-chasing fools.

12. The Futility of Life Itself

Ecclesiastes 6:1-12

[1] There is an evil which I have seen under the sun and it is prevalent among men—[2] a man to whom God has given riches and wealth and honor so that his soul lacks nothing of all that he desires; yet God has not empowered him to eat from them, for a foreigner enjoys them. This is vanity and a severe affliction. [3] If a man fathers a hundred children and lives many years, however many they may be, but his soul is not satisfied with good things and he does not even have a proper burial, then I say, "Better the miscarriage than he, [4] for it comes in futility and goes into obscurity; and its name is covered in obscurity. [5] It never sees the sun and it never knows anything; it is better off than he. [6] Even if the other man lives a thousand years twice and does not enjoy good things—do not all go to one place?"

[7] All a man's labor is for his mouth and yet the appetite is not satisfied. [8] For what advantage does the wise man have over the fool? What advantage does the poor man have, knowing how to walk before the living? [9] What the eyes see is better than what the soul desires. This too is futility and a striving after wind.

[10] Whatever exists has already been named, and it is known what man is; for he cannot dispute with him who is stronger than he is. [11] For there are many words which increase futility. What then is the advantage to a man? [12] For who knows what is good for a man during his lifetime, during the few years of his futile life? He will spend them like a shadow. For who can tell a man what will be after him under the sun?

In the previous verses the Preacher addresses those to whom God has not only given riches, but also the power to enjoy them (5:19). He now turns to those to whom God has given power and honor but *not* the ability to enjoy them (6:2). In Ecclesiastes 6:1-6, R. N. Whybray observes, the Preacher is "not so much presenting concrete examples to illustrate his theme as reflecting on various hypothetical circumstances, no doubt based on real cases, in which the possession of those supposed advantages in life most prized by traditional wisdom teaching—wealth, social position, a large family, long life (the gifts of wisdom according to Prov. 3:16 and 8:18)—proves ultimately valueless" (Whybray, p. 104).

Once again God is center stage. According to the Preacher, "unless God grants it, man can have *nothing*. Contrary to the American dream, there is no such creature as the self-made man" (Ehlke, p. 57). Beyond the basic fact that it is God who bestows wealth and honor, it is equally true that He gives us the power to enjoy those gifts (6:2).

The point the Preacher is making is that it is possible to possess things without enjoying them. Roland Ehlke illustrates the point by noting that "TV soap operas frequently depict this kind of individual. He's rich and powerful, but because of his selfishness and greed he's caught in one frustrating situation after another. The viewer rarely, if ever, sees him enjoying his vast possessions" (*ibid.,* p. 58).

Verse 2 tells us that one reason that rich people might fail to enjoy their wealth is that a foreigner has apparently taken it away from them. The word translated as "foreigner" or "stranger" (RSV) can mean "someone who is not a member of one's family" (Lohfink, p. 86).

Several possible pictures come to mind as we think of an outsider grasping another's wealth. An inventor, for example, develops a new product but lacks marketing savvy. He invites in a partner to do that part of the task only to see the slick marketer steal the rights. Other cases suggest physical theft or even identity theft, but the result is always the same. One person has struggled to gather the wealth, only to see another enjoy the fruits of hard labor. The sad fact of life is that wealth can be taken from hard working innocent people even before their death. The newspapers are full of accounts of scam artists who specialize in separating the elderly from their money. As the Preacher well knew, it is an ugly world that we live in. Please note that it is not God who is behind such people, but by His grace He continues to allow them to live not only to demonstrate the fruits of evil but in the hope that they might come to repentance (2 Peter 3:9).

Such a world, viewed from a human perspective, especially that of someone who had been ripped off twice, appears to be meaningless (Eccl. 6:2b). The preacher goes on in verses 3 to 6 to reflect on the problem of a person not being able to enjoy God's gifts. He illustrates his point that even if a person had 100 children and lived an extremely long life (2,000 years in verse 6) but remains dissatisfied it is all futility. (Having lots of children who would survive to take care of them in old age was a fundamental concern in the ancient world.)

Such persons would have been better off, the Preacher suggests, if their mothers had miscarried or they had been still-born. At least then they would not have had to hassle through life only to end up dissatisfied and disrespected. What is the use of going through the pain of life if one cannot enjoy it? Another way of making the Preacher's point in Ecclesiastes 6:3-6 is to realize that the quality of life is more important than its quantity. Life is meaningless unless it brings satisfaction and pleasure.

In verse 6 our author is winding up again on his long-life-is-fruitless argument only to stop in midstream and ask the obvious: "do not all go to one place?" Here we have a reflection intruding on a reflection. In Ecclesiastes 5:18-20 he had held that those who had good things ought to enjoy them, while in the first six verses of chapter 6 he emphasized what a disaster it was for a person to have good things and not enjoy them. But now at the end of verse 6 he comes back to the basic fact that all die and go to the grave whether they have found pleasure in life or not. That utter fact was the ultimate issue from the Preacher's under the sun perspective. To him enjoyment was good but it had its limits. It could never be an ultimate good because of the ever grasping reality of the tomb, the factor that made everything else under the sun meaningless in the long run.

In verse 7-10 we find a cluster of proverbs related to verses 1-6. The first (verse 7) tells us that even though "a man's labor is for his mouth" yet "the appetite is not satisfied." That proverb seemingly stands in tension with the Preacher's admonition in Ecclesiastes 5:18-20 to eat, drink, and enjoy life. The implication probably is that even though those pleasures are the best that life has to offer, they are still not enough. Such activities are the most that we can hope for in this life, but the plain fact is that in and of themselves they do not make a life always marching toward the grave (6:6) ultimately meaningful. We may strive and strain in this under the sun world but that struggle will never fill us or bring us a satisfactory meaning for our existence.

The second proverb (verse 8) is difficult to understand. The first half, "what advantage does the wise man have over the fool?" is clear enough. The Preacher has touched upon this topic before and concluded that there is none since both individuals end up in the grave (2:14-17). But the second part, the one dealing with the poor, as David Hubbard puts it, "has caused scholars to wring their hands in frustration." His best guess at its meaning is that we should interpret the second half of the verse as a complement to the first half. Thus, given the grave's "appetite, neither the wise nor the fool can escape it. Furthermore, even poor people, who overcome hardship to live a productive and respectable life, cannot enjoy any ultimate advantage. They too will end up in Sheol's belly" (Hubbard, *Ecclesiastes,* p. 154).

Verse 9, the third proverb, states that "what the eyes see is better than what the soul desires." The Good News Translation brings out the implications of the verse nicely: "It is better to be satisfied with what you have than to be always wanting something else." A more contemporary saying is "a bird in the hand is better than two in the bush." That sentiment echoes Ecclesiastes' repeated emphasis on the present as opposed to the future.

But in the end, life is a futile pursuit after the wind. Here the Preacher uses the vanity/meaningless/absurd verdict in its full form for the final time. The last six chapters of his book will tend to focus more on such questions as that found in Ecclesiastes 6:12: "For who knows what is good for a man during his lifetime . . . ?"

The major purpose of Ecclesiastes 6:10-12 is to highlight the limits of human freedom. The Preacher has already demonstrated that there is really nothing new under the sun and that humans can do nothing to change the shape of reality (10a; cf. 1:4-11; 3:1-15), but he now adds in the second half of verse 10 that it is useless to dispute with God, who is stronger than us. In verse 11 he advances the idea that endless talking won't solve our problems or ultimately alter things.

Then in verse 12 he sets forth two questions that set the stage for the rest of his book:

1. "For who knows what is good for a man during his lifetime, during the few years of his futile life?"

2. "For who can tell a man what will be after him under the sun?"

The implied answer to both questions is "certainly not human beings." Their life is like a flitting shadow racing across the earth. The sad fact is that humans who live under the sun do not have the answers to the meaning of life. From an earthly perspective, as the Preacher has repeatedly demonstrated, life looks meaningless.

Whether we like it or not, Michael Eaton observes, "the Preacher is slamming every door, except the door of faith" (Eaton, p. 108). We can tell neither "what is good" nor "what will be" (6:12). Step by step the Preacher is leading his readers to see that the only answer to life's meaning has to do with God.

13. Some Better Thans

Ecclesiastes 7:1–22
>^{1}*A good name is better than a good*
>   *ointment,*
>*And the day of one's death is*
>   *better than the day of one's birth.*
>^{2}*It is better to go to a house of*
>   *mourning*
>*Than to go to a house of feasting,*
>*Because that is the end of every man,*
>*And the living takes it to heart.*
>^{3}*Sorrow is better than laughter,*
>*For when a face is sad a heart*
>   *may be happy.*
>^{4}*The mind of the wise is in the*
>   *house of mourning,*
>*While the mind of fools is in the*
>   *house of pleasure.*
>^{5}*It is better to listen to the rebuke*
>   *of a wise man*
>*Than for one to listen to the song*
>   *of fools.*
>^{6}*For as the crackling of thorn*
>   *bushes under a pot,*
>*So is the laughter of the fool;*
>*And this too is futility.*
>^{7}*For oppression makes a wise*
>   *man mad,*
>*And a bribe corrupts the heart.*

⁸*The end of a matter is better than*
*   its beginning;*
Patience of spirit is better than
*   haughtiness of spirit.*
⁹*Do not be eager in your heart to*
*   be angry,*
For anger resides in the bosom of
*   fools.*
¹⁰*Do not say, "Why is it that the*
*   former days were better than these?"*
For it is not from wisdom that
*   you ask about this.*
¹¹*Wisdom along with an inheritance*
*   is good*
And an advantage to those who see the sun.
¹²*For wisdom is protection just as*
*   money is protection,*
But the advantage of knowledge
*   is that wisdom preserves the*
*   lives of its possessors.*
¹³*Consider the work of God,*
For who is able to straighten
*   what He has bent?*
¹⁴*In the day of prosperity be*
*   happy,*
But in the day of adversity
*   consider—*
God has made the one as well as
*   the other*
So that man will not discover
*   anything that will be after him.*

¹⁵*I have seen everything during my lifetime of futility; there is a righteous man who perishes in his righteousness and there is a wicked man who prolongs his life in his wickedness.* ¹⁶*Do not be excessively righteous and do not be overly wise. Why should you ruin yourself?* ¹⁷*Do not be excessively wicked and do not be a fool. Why should you die before your time?* ¹⁸*It is good that you grasp one thing and also not let go of the other; for the one who fears God comes forth with both of them.*

¹⁹*Wisdom strengthens a wise man more than ten rulers who are in a city.* ²⁰*Indeed, there is not a righteous man on earth who continually does good and who never sins.* ²¹*Also, do not take seriously all words which are spoken, so that you will not hear your servant cursing you.* ²²*For you also*

have realized that you likewise have many times cursed others.

With Ecclesiastes 7:1-14 we come to a collection of proverbs that center on a series of general themes:

1. Solemnity is better than levity (verses 1-7)
2. Patience is better than haste (verses 8-10)
3. Wisdom with wealth is better than wisdom alone (verses 11, 12)
4. Resignation is better than indignation (verses 13, 14)

Closely connected in thought with verses 13 and 14, which focus on God's sovereign ways, are verses 15-22, which form a fifth "better than":

5. Moderation is better than intemperance (verses 15-22).

We will examine this rather complex section of Ecclesiastes by looking at each "better than" sequentially. The best that we can say of verses 1-7 is that they are not very cheerful. Verse 1 starts out all right. Declaring that "a good name is better than a good ointment" is positive enough. It is in fact common Near Eastern wisdom. "A good name," we read in Proverbs 22:1, "is to be more desired than great wealth." Traditional wisdom valued highly a person's reputation. The Preacher had no problem with that.

But, as Derek Kidner points out, "nothing in the first half of verse 1 prepares us for the body-blow of the second half" (Kidner, *Message,* p. 64). To say that "the day of one's death is better than the day of one's birth" is distinctively Ecclesiastes and contrary to traditional wisdom, which held for the blessedness of a long life.

It is the negative second half of verse 1 that sets the stage for verses 2-4 with their thought that mourning is better than feasting (death being the ultimate end of every person, verse 2), sorrow being better than laughter (verse 3), and that wise peoples' minds should dwell in the house of mourning rather than in that of pleasure (verse 4).

The lesson the Preacher seems to have in mind is that it is important for people to come to grips with the ultimate realities of life rather than to follow the escapist path of a pleasure-bent course that merely anesthetizes them to the bitter facts of a less than perfect existence. In the house of mourning the mood is thoughtful as people stand face to face with the undeniable fact of death. Psalm 90, which treats human mortality, sets forth the same lesson as Ecclesiastes 7:1-4. Speaking of God, it says,

"Teach us to number our days
that we may get a heart of wisdom" (verse 12, RSV).

Iain Provan perceptively writes that "death is an evangelist." It helps us see our need and come to grips with who we are in contrast to who God is (Provan, pp. 147, 148). It is in that sense that the Preacher can say that it is better to be in the house of mourning. Death forces us to think.

Ecclesiastes 7:5 and 6 continue the same theme as verses 1-4, with the thought that the burning of thorn bushes under a pot reminds one of the laughter of a fool. James Crenshaw notes that "thistles provide quick flames, little heat, and a lot of unpleasant noise" (Crenshaw, *Ecclesiastes*, p. 135). So is the conversation of a fool. It lacks the substance of solid thought.

"Death is an evangelist."

With verses 8-10 we enter a line of thought emphasizing that patience is better than haste. The Preacher advocates a calm attitude and lifestyle. Provan sums up verses 8 and 9 by noting that "a wise person will not react immediately to circumstances but will take a longer term view, waiting to see the full measure of a matter before deciding how to respond. It is the fool who arrogantly or angrily makes an immediate response (cf. Prov. 12:16; 14:29), giving speedy expression to the anger that has been nursed" (Provan, p. 141).

It is not altogether clear how verse 10 relates to verses 8 and 9, but the longing for the past may be a specific example of the impatience of those in verses 8 and 9 who fail to adequately understand that things in an under the sun kind of world never have been good. Those who long for the good old days when everything was as it should be are simply ignorant of history. A person only has to read the historical sections of the Bible or old newspapers to realize the truthfulness of Otto Bettmann's book, *The Good Old Days—They Were Terrible!* It has been so since the Genesis Fall. To think otherwise, the Preacher claims, is not the way of wisdom (verse 10). The path of wisdom, we noted in Ecclesiastes 7:1-6, leads away from pipe dreams and toward the ultimate facts of reality.

Ecclesiastes 7:11, 12 transport us to a third "better than": wisdom with wealth is better than wisdom alone. While there is nothing especially revolutionary in saying that "wisdom along with an inheritance is good," the fact that the Preacher links that thought with an allusion to seeing the sun brings our minds back to his ever present theme of mortality. After all, one day the darkness of death sweeps over us and we will no longer see the sun, no matter how rich we might be. In the meantime, wisdom guides and protects those with money as they navigate through life (see verse 12).

Verses 13 and 14 help us recognize that resignation to the will of God is better than indignation in the face of those things that mortal humans cannot change. With its council to accept in stride both the good times and the bad, verse 14 is a classic statement regarding how to have a healthy life in a world whose general course we are helpless to change. As one author puts it, "Man cannot foresee his future, nor can he altogether control circumstances in which he may be involved. Consequently it is man's privilege to trust God and submit to His will, assured that in His hands all will work together for good (Rom. 8:28; cf. Gen. 42:36)" (Nichol, vol. 3, p. 1088). To put it bluntly, we as humans are not as self sufficient as we would like to be. We need to learn to accept what cannot be changed and get on with our lives rather than to resist endlessly as we walk the path of ceaseless ulcers.

Ecclesiastes 7:15 appears to be a specific example of the teaching of verse 14 that people cannot control what comes their way—whether adversity or prosperity. More specifically, verse 15 points out that neither the righteous nor the wicked always get their just desserts on this earth. The wise sage of Proverbs may claim that "the fear of the Lord prolongs days, but the years of the wicked will be shortened" (Prov. 10:27, NKJV), but the Preacher knows for a fact that it doesn't always work out that way in our under the sun world. He has "seen" the opposite with his own eyes (Eccl. 7:15).

In that context the Preacher warns against arrogant wisdom and self-righteousness (see Whybray, p. 120, for arguments that the wisdom and righteousness discussed in verse 16 are distorted rather than balanced), which lead to ruin. Michael Eaton sums up verses 16 and 17 by suggesting that "the right life walks the path between two extremes, shunning self-righteousness, but not allowing one's native wickedness to run its own course" (Eaton, p. 114). After all, unbridled wickedness only increases the risk of an untimely death (Eccl. 7:17; cf. Ps. 55:23).

Ecclesiastes 7:18 advises the wise person to hold onto the admonitions of the two previous verses. And verse 19 in its context tells us that wisdom, even with all its weaknesses in an under the sun world, is a powerful force. Verses 20-22 offer a final dose of the Preacher's realism in three short statements:

1. None of us under the sun people are altogether good (verse 20).
2. We should not take ourselves or even what other people say about us too seriously (verse 21).
3. After all, we haven't always respected others in our words and actions (verse 22).

In summary, Ecclesiastes 7:1-22 does not present a happy picture. But the passage sets forth a realistic one of people living a life under the sun. In this passage the Preacher offers an excellent analysis of the problems of life but provides no ultimate solutions.

But don't worry. He is heading in that direction as he moves toward the climax of his thought provoking book. And where he leaves off the New Testament will pick up. If the Preacher appears to have a message of no hope, he does point us to our need of the hope that we can only find in Jesus Christ.

14. More Words of Advice

Ecclesiastes 7:23-8:9

²³I tested all this with wisdom, and I said, "I will be wise," but it was far from me. ²⁴What has been is remote and exceedingly mysterious. Who can discover it? ²⁵I directed my mind to know, to investigate and to seek wisdom and an explanation, and to know the evil of folly and the foolishness of madness. ²⁶And I discovered more bitter than death the woman whose heart is snares and nets, whose hands are chains. One who is pleasing to God will escape from her, but the sinner will be captured by her. ²⁷"Behold, I have discovered this," says the Preacher, "adding one thing to another to find an explanation, ²⁸which I am still seeking but have not found. I have found one man among a thousand, but I have not found a woman among all these. ²⁹Behold, I have found only this, that God made men upright, but they have sought out many devices."

8 Who is like the wise man and who knows the interpretation of a matter? A man's wisdom illumines him and causes his stern face to beam.

²I say, "Keep the command of the king because of the oath before God. ³Do not be in a hurry to leave him. Do not join in an evil matter, for he will do whatever he pleases." ⁴Since the word of the king is authoritative, who will say to him, "What are you doing?"

⁵He who keeps a royal command experiences no trouble, for a wise heart knows the proper time and procedure. ⁶For there is a proper time and procedure for every delight, though a man's trouble is heavy upon him. ⁷If no one knows what will happen, who can tell him when it will happen? ⁸No man has authority to restrain the wind with the wind, or authority over the day of death; and there is no discharge in the time of war, and evil will not deliver those who practice it. ⁹All this I have seen and applied my mind to every deed that has been done under the sun wherein a man has exercised authority over another to his hurt.

I sympathize with the Preacher when he reports that he determined to be wise, tested everything with wisdom, and came up disappointed (Eccl. 7:23). My own life's journey has been similar to his. In my agnostic years I sought meaning in pleasure (hedonism), only to find it empty in the end. I then vigorously sought ultimate purpose through a rather human-centered perfectionistic approach to religion that left me devastated in a sea of frustration. At that point, as I noted in section 3, I resigned from the ministry and sought meaning in philosophy, only to come to the same conclusion as the Preacher. After six years of grappling with the thoughts of the world's greatest minds I concluded that human philosophy held no final answers and that the wisdom I sought was still "far from me."

The Preacher and I are not alone in our mission. You, my friend, find yourself in the same boat. Every person struggles with the issue of meaning and significance even though we may approach our search from various directions and utilize different avenues of investigation. But we not only share the same quest, if we are honest we also arrive at the same conclusion as did the author of Ecclesiastes when it comes to the unaided human (under the sun) search for meaning.

Back in Ecclesiastes 1:13 the Preacher "tells us that he had embarked on a voyage of exploration to discover the meaning of all that goes on in life. He had journeyed to strange lands and had come up with some unexpected conclusions. He now gives us his considered verdict on the voyage. The object of his journey, that treasure of wisdom which could provide the key to unlock the secret of what life is all about, has proven elusive. He has searched, he has failed to find. It remains forever beyond his grasp, deep, 'deeper than man can fathom' (v. 24, NEB)" (Davidson, p. 53).

His quest reminds us of the discussion on the acquisition of wisdom in Job 28:

> "But where shall wisdom be found?
> And where is the place of understanding?
> Man does not know the way to it,
>   and it is not found in the land of the living"
> (verses 12, 13, RSV).

In Ecclesiastes 7:25 the Preacher again reminds us that he determined "to investigate and to seek wisdom and an explanation." Then in verses 26 through 28 he alerts us to the specific subjects of his investigation—men and women.

First he reports his conclusions on women, finding them to be "more bitter than death" (verse 26). Many students of Ecclesiastes have sought to restrict his findings on those women whose "heart is snares" to those passages in Proverbs that treat the adulterous "strange" woman who is like "a deep pit" that men fall into (Prov. 22:14; 23:27), but in verse 28 the Preacher tells us that he means all women. None passed his wisdom test.

According to his description of his methodology, the Preacher did not make a casual investigation. He added "one thing to another to find an explanation" (Eccl. 7:27). Michael Fox notes that he carefully studied "the opposite sex with an accountant's eye" only to find that "it doesn't add up" (Fox, *A Time to Tear Down*, p. 270).

Now one doesn't have to be a rocket scientist to realize that the Preacher's conclusions are not politically correct according to modern standards. He reminds us of the early Church Father who noted that Satan, after stripping Job of all that was precious to him, left him his wife "because Satan thought that she would greatly assist him in conquering this saint of God" (Davidson, p. 54).

But if the Preacher had a negative view of women, he wasn't much more positive about men. While it is true that not a single female passed his test, he only found "one man among a thousand" who could do so (Eccl. 7:28). That is, only one-tenth of one percent of males met his approval. Thus his evaluation of males was more positive than that of females, but only marginally so.

The question naturally arises, "What conclusions can we draw from these verses?" First, he wasn't against women as such, which we see from Ecclesiastes 9:9 ("Enjoy life with the woman whom you love"). Second, the evaluation of Ecclesiastes 7.26-28 is in the context of those who have achieved some level of wisdom. As Fox points out, "of a thousand people, Qohelet found one *real* human; the rest were dumb animals. And these rare people turned out to be all males, for, looking at the one-in-a-thousand, he found not so much as one woman." Fox goes on to note that one subjective fact in his evaluation was that the Preacher understood males better than men (Fox, *A Time to Tear Down*, p. 271). Perhaps we have here a case in point of the differences between males and females set forth in John Gray's popular *Men Are From Mars, Women Are From Venus*. At any rate, the Preacher is offering his subjective opinion. We should not view his evaluation as ultimate fact any more than many of the rambling remarks in the book of Job. The Preacher even goes so far as to claim that he hasn't come to any final conclusion on the matter, but is "still seeking" and investigating the topic (Eccl. 7:28).

On the other hand, he willingly declares one conclusion without hesitation. He states in no uncertain terms in verse 29 "that God made men upright, but they have sought out many devices."

That verse makes two crucial points. First, it is not God's fault that people are messed up. Reflecting on Genesis 1 and 2, the Preacher notes that God made people "upright." We best appreciate the importance of that teaching when we contrast it with such documents as the Babylonian Theodicy, which depicts the gods as responsible for human wickedness (see Kidner, *Message,* p. 73). W. Sibley Towner notes that even though some passages in Ecclesiastes lean toward divine predetermination (e.g., 6:10; 7:14), "even Qohelet makes theological allowance for human freedom and, therefore, for human error and malfeasance, for which human being's must be deemed responsible" (Towner, p. 332).

The second crucial point in Ecclesiastes 7:29 is that humans "have sought out many devices." Here we find allusion to Genesis 3-6, especially Genesis 6:5: "The Lord saw that the wickedness of man was great in the earth, and that every imagination of the thoughts of his heart was only evil continually" (RSV). The word translated as "thoughts" in that verse comes from the same Hebrew root as "devices" in Ecclesiastes 7:29. In short, while the Preacher held that a very small percentage of humans had attained wisdom (verses 27, 28), he was quite certain that none were morally upright (verse 29). It is apparently such a conclusion that brings a sense of satisfaction to the "wise man" and causes his face to shine (8:1).

In Ecclesiastes 8:2-6 we find the Preacher's thoughts about how to survive when serving in the court of the king. He has no doubt about the king's authority, and both secular history and the biblical picture indicate that Near Eastern monarchs had almost absolute power over their subjects. The king held power that even the wise needed to respect.

It is in that context that Ecclesiastes provides a short manual on how to deal with royalty and not get into trouble.

1. Obey his commands (verses 2, 5).
2. Don't double cross him, since he does whatever pleases him (such as, squelch a coup, verse 3).
3. Don't foolishly question his actions (verse 4).
4. Utilize whatever wisdom you possess to observe proper times and procedures (verses 5, 6).

Please note that Ecclesiastes 8:2-6 does not raise the delicate topic of civil disobedience faced by Daniel and his three friends (Dan. 3, 6; cf. Acts 5:29). Nor does the passage present us with a theory of the state. Rather, it gives some general guidelines on how to succeed in government service.

One prominent feature in verses 2-6 is the king's power and authority. But the Preacher does not regard royal authority as absolute. To the contrary, in verses 7 and 8 he lists five major human limitations that apply even to royalty.

> **Five Limitations on Human Authority**
> 1. No one knows the future.
> 2. No one can control the wind.
> 3. No one can prevent death.
> 4. No one can get out of a battle.
> 5. No one can be delivered by their evil.

They warn even the most powerful of humans (verse 9) that we can afford to be humble in the face of forces that affect all of our lives yet are beyond our control. Such are some of the under the sun realities that wise people need to seriously ponder. The Preacher hasn't fully shown his hand with an above the sun answer to those realities, but he is advancing slowly but certainly in that direction.

15. Life Is Full of Uncertainties

Ecclesiastes 8:10-17

> *¹⁰So then, I have seen the wicked buried, those who used to go in and out from the holy place, and they are soon forgotten in the city where they did thus. This too is futility. ¹¹Because the sentence against an evil deed is not executed quickly, therefore the hearts of the sons of men among them are given fully to do evil. ¹²Although a sinner does evil a hundred times and may lengthen his life, still I know that it will be well for those who fear God, who fear Him openly. ¹³But it will not be well for the evil man and he will not lengthen his days like a shadow because he does not fear God.*
>
> *¹⁴There is futility which is done on the earth, that is, there are righteous men to whom it happens according to the deeds of the wicked. On the other hand, there are evil men to whom it happens according to the deeds of the righteous. I say that this too is futility. ¹⁵So I commended pleasure, for there is nothing good for a man under the sun except to eat and to drink and to be merry, and this will stand by him in his toils throughout the days of his life which God has given him under the sun.*
>
> *¹⁶When I gave my heart to know wisdom and to see the task which has been done on the earth (even though one should never sleep day or night), ¹⁷and I saw every work of God, I concluded that man cannot discover the work which has been done under the sun. Even though man should seek laboriously, he will not discover; and though the wise man should say, "I know," he cannot discover.*

Some television programs are just plain upsetting. David Hubbard recalls an Alfred Hitchcock program that he has never been able to forget. The program "began with a couple chatting cordially as they drove through a country town. Their peaceful drive was interrupted by the shriek of a siren and the flashing of lights behind them. As they slowed their car in response, the police vehicle lurched past them and then cut in front of them forcing their car into a low concrete wall at the edge of the road.

"In shock they climbed out and discovered the bump had broken their right front wheel. They turned to protest the matter to the policemen who were now at their side, when one of the burly cops slugged the bewildered man in the face. 'You saw him start to swing at me, didn't you?' he growled at his partner, whose surly response was, 'I sure did!'"

Hubbard reports that he and his wife "could feel our outrage heat to the boiling point and beyond as [we] watched the next scene unfold. The tow truck came along and hauled the car to the garage where an unearthly fee was quoted for the towing and repairs. The incensed couple was dragged to the office of the Justice of the Peace where all their protests fell on deaf ears and an exorbitant fine was levied for their alleged speeding and attempted assault. It was obvious that the whole crew—police, truck driver, mechanic, and judge—were in cahoots." The Hubbards "watched in disbelief as the shattered couple, demeaned, defrauded, and downcast, climbed into the car to make their way out of that wicked town." Everything in them cried out, "'That's not fair. Life ought not to be that way. Is there no justice to be found?'"

The characters continued on in despair and hopelessness. "Then as the couple eased their way out of town, the man asked the woman, 'Did you get all that?' She opened her purse, pulled out a compact tape recorder, and began to replay the entire scenario. . . . The couple were government agents investigating reports of speed-trap rackets in the small town. They had their hard evidence. Vindication was on the way" (Hubbard, *Ecclesiastes*, pp. 189, 190).

The problem of justice and injustice deeply perplexed the Preacher. In Ecclesiastes 8:10 he reports that he had seen certain wicked religious hypocrites receive a reward they didn't deserve. That rather complex and difficult verse to translate echoes the sentiment of Ecclesiastes 4:1 and 5:8, in which those in a position of power and authority oppress the weak. Our author is more than aware of the fact that he lived in a messed up world. But it isn't mere wickedness that bothers him in Ecclesiastes 8:10. It is that he had witnessed hypocrites receiving rewards *because* of their hypocrisy.

"There are few things more obnoxious than the sight of wicked men flourishing and complacent. Yet wickedness respected and given the blessing of religion (10a) is even more sickening" (Kidner, *Message,* pp. 76, 77).

But rewarded wickedness is only part of the problem. Verse 11 raises questions about God. Why isn't He doing His job? His lack of quick retribution only makes things worse. People watch, witness the unpunished wicked prosper, and commit themselves "fully to do evil." "The lag in retribution," Gaius Atkins asserts, "is the secret of many of our follies and our faults. It lulls us into a false sense of security. If evil, like fire, scorched us at once, we would take care; but when its issues are hidden by time—?" (Atkins, p. 71). The Preacher was well aware of that truth. God's failure to respond quickly bothered him.

But though he had "seen" the wicked rewarded (Eccl. 8:10) there were some other things that he also "knew" to be true (verse 12). The Preacher knew beyond a shadow of a doubt that in the end God would set things right. He knew that God in His own time would honor those who fear Him and that the wicked would receive what they deserved. In verses 12 and 13 he seems to not only be implying a final judgment (cf. 12:14) but also that even on earth a good life still generally gets rewarded and a wicked life generally penalized.

But still he had seen exceptions to the general rule, and they bothered him greatly. Thus he raises the whole issue of the righteous receiving the just reward of the wicked and vice versa in verse 14.

The Preacher lived in the tension between what he knew about the ultimate justice of God and what he saw all too often in daily life. He would have agreed with the sentiments of Longfellow:

"Though the mills of God grind slowly,
    yet they grind exceeding small;
Though with patience he stand waiting,
    with exactness grinds he all."

While the Preacher would have approved the poet's sentiment, the divine patience still bothered him. Things would be a whole lot better, our author thought, if God dealt with evil immediately and gave everybody what they deserved without any delay. Why didn't He act? How can we make sense out of a world that appears to lack meaning? Life is absurd. It is no accident that verse 14 begins and ends with the word "futility." From an under the sun perspective that is the Preacher's major conclusion at the end of eight chapters of investigation.

How thinking people can live in such a world and retain some sanity is the issue that he faces in verse 15. He provides his readers with no formula for understanding the mysteries of God, but he does offer what he believes is the God-given solution for coping with a less than perfect world. Once again he says that the best way to maintain our equilibrium in a messed up world is to eat, drink, and enjoy God's gifts. That advice is not new. Previously he offered it in Ecclesiastes 2:24, 25; 3:12-13, 22; and 5:18-20. He recognizes that pleasure does not hold any ultimate answers (2:2), but he is also convicted that enjoying God's gifts is important to people struggling with the meaning of life and the mysteries of God (see section 7 for a discussion of this recurring theme).

One wonders if the Preacher is able to follow his own coping advice. Quickly he breezes through the enjoy life advice of verse 15 and plunges back into his obsessive searching for meaning in verses 16 and 17. But by now even he is ready to conclude finally that life's significance in the face of a mixed up unjust world is undiscoverable. He has spent ceaseless days and sleepless nights (verse 16) in his quest, but his final conclusion is that "man cannot discover" the ultimate answer. Even if "the wise man should say, 'I know,'" he really doesn't (verse 17). Thus "the Teacher's great discovery about the nature of God's activity ('then I saw all that God has done') is that he does not comprehend it" (Garrett, p. 330). The Preacher has said the same thing before, but this time he asserts it with an air of finality. After Ecclesiastes 8:16, 17 he ceases to mention his personal quest. Subsequent to a discussion of the uncertainty of life and the absolute certainty of death (9:1-12) he spends most of the rest of his time providing advice for living in our under the sun world (9:13-12:7).

The first eight chapters of Ecclesiastes is a failed quest for a human (under the sun) philosophic understanding of ultimate meaning. The Preacher will move beyond this approach in Ecclesiastes' last chapter. But for the most complete understanding of the meaning of human life in the face of certain death the world would have to await the advent of Jesus who bore the fullness of the revelation of God (Heb. 1:1–3), who Himself was not only "the way, and the truth, and the life" (John 14:6), but who had also won the victory over death (1 Cor. 15). The lesson of the Preacher is that human thought will never lead us to a satisfactory view of truth. The true answers to the riddle of life lie in God's gift of revelation to the human race.

16. But Death Is Certain

Ecclesiastes 9:1-12

¹For I have taken all this to my heart and explain it that righteous men, wise men, and their deeds are in the hand of God. Man does not know whether it will be love or hatred; anything awaits him.

²It is the same for all. There is one fate for the righteous and for the wicked; for the good, for the clean and for the unclean; for the man who offers a sacrifice and for the one who does not sacrifice. As the good man is, so is the sinner; as the swearer is, so is the one who is afraid to swear. ³This is an evil in all that is done under the sun, that there is one fate for all men. Furthermore, the hearts of the sons of men are full of evil and insanity is in their hearts throughout their lives. Afterwards they go to the dead. ⁴For whoever is joined with all the living, there is hope; surely a live dog is better than a dead lion. ⁵For the living know they will die; but the dead do not know anything, nor have they any longer a reward, for their memory is forgotten. ⁶Indeed their love, their hate and their zeal have already perished, and they will no longer have a share in all that is done under the sun.

⁷Go then, eat your bread in happiness and drink your wine with a cheerful heart; for God has already approved your works. ⁸Let your clothes be white all the time, and let not oil be lacking on your head. ⁹Enjoy life with the woman whom you love all the days of your fleeting life which He has given to you under the sun; for this is your reward in life and in your toil in which you have labored under the sun.

¹⁰Whatever your hand finds to do, do it with all your might; for there is no activity or planning or knowledge or wisdom in Sheol where you are going.

¹¹"I again saw under the sun that the race is not to the swift and the battle is not to the warriors, and neither is bread to the wise nor wealth to

the discerning nor favor to men of ability; for time and chance overtake them all. [12]Moreover, man does not know his time: like fish caught in a treacherous net and birds trapped in a snare, so the sons of men are ensnared at an evil time when it suddenly falls on them.

The law of the tombstone is universal: sooner or later everybody gets one. Before moving on to the more positive counsel of his last three chapters, in Ecclesiastes 9:1-12 the Preacher, in case any haven't gotten the message yet, nails the door shut on any false hopes. "A lengthening shadow extends throughout the book," writes James Crenshaw, "becoming especially dark in this unit. Qohelet thinks no one can ascertain the deity's disposition toward humans, for a common fate befalls everyone regardless of religious performance or its absence" (Crenshaw, *Ecclesiastes*, p. 159).

In verse 1 we find him donning his thinking cap again. Once more he reminds us that our fate rests in the hand of God. But he adds that he doesn't know if the basic principle of the universe is love or hate. And from an under the sun perspective he is right. The natural world in itself doesn't help us understand God's nature or even the tilt of His creation. We might exclaim that the natural world is one of love and peace as we sit quietly in the park and watch a mother squirrel romp with her half-grown young. Then a cat springs from hiding and snatches one of them, leaving us to mutter about the destruction and death and hatred of the natural order. The Preacher has also observed that reality. From a human perspective he is not so sure if love or hatred awaits individuals (verse 1). But, on the other hand, he is absolutely certain that death will get every last one of them (verses 2-6).

And the disgusting thing is that it doesn't seem to matter how good or bad or how religious or irreligious people have been (verse 2). Life has "one fate for all men" (verse 3). "Equal fates for unequal persons," Michael Fox observes, "is an absurdity from which not even the fortunate are exempt" (Fox, *A Time to Tear Down*, p. 292). Such is "an evil." It is "as wrong as anything that happens in this world. As long as people live, their minds are full of evil and madness, and suddenly they die" (verse 3, TEV). And that means everybody—even you, even the truly and genuinely good person. We all, each and every one of us, end up at tombstone junction.

By now it is no secret to the readers of Ecclesiastes that death dominates his every thought. The injustice of it all frustrates him so much that he now blatantly contradicts himself. This man who had earlier "congratulated the dead who are already dead more than the living" (4:2) and declared that "the day of one's death is better than the day of one's birth" (7:1) now tells us that it is better to be a "live dog" than "a dead lion" (9:4). To get his full meaning, we need to remember that people in the ancient world despised dogs while viewing lions as the most princely of beasts.

At least, the Preacher observes, a living person has some hope and knowledge. But when all is said and done that is a mighty slim advantage, since all the living really know is that they shall die, while the dead know absolutely nothing (verse 5).

Ecclesiastes 9:5, contrary to what many believe, is not speaking about the human condition in death as being like a deep sleep. That concept surfaces in Daniel 12:2; John 11:11-13; 1 Thessalonians 4:13, 14, and other places. But in Ecclesiastes 9:5 the Preacher is teaching that from a purely human under the sun perspective death is the end of the line. He has already told us that both people and animals end up in the same place—the grave—and that there is "no advantage for man over beast. . . . All go to the same place." "Who knows," he asks, "that the breath of man ascends upward and the breath of the beast descends downward to the earth?" Humans are nothing "but beasts" (3:18-20).

> ### A Humanistic View of Death
>
> "I was . . . sure of my present life and of the death that was coming. That, no doubt, was all I had; but at least that certainty was something I could get my teeth into—just as it had got its teeth into me" (Camus, *The Stranger,* p. 151).

H. C. Leupold makes an important point about the Preacher's approach to death when he writes that "it seems that interpreters have not fully grasped the meaning of the phrase which is here [9:3, 6] so carefully inserted—'under the sun.' That always implies leaving out of consideration all higher values and divine factors and limiting oneself exclusively to values and facts that the natural man can apprehend." Thus Leupold argues that we have no right to consider these verses to be the Preacher's full opinion on the state of the dead (Leupold, pp. 209, 211).

Be that as it may, the Preacher in all of his discussions leaves people with nothing but a silent grave. We need to go elsewhere in the Old Testament to find a glimmer of the resurrection. The clearest reference is Daniel 12:2: "Many of those who sleep in the dust of the earth shall awake, some to everlasting life, and some to shame and everlasting contempt" (RSV; cf. Isa. 26:19; Job 19:25-27). Even in the Old Testament a massive gap exists between an under the sun perspective and an above the sun viewpoint.

The Preacher shifts moods in Ecclesiastes 9:7-10. In verses 2-6 he presented us with the dirge of death, but now he once again suggests his alternate conclusion. As Roland Ehlke puts it, "death is certain. Life is short. Once you've gone, you'll never return to live on this earth. Why, then, waste time fretting over things you can't control? 'Enjoy life,' urges the Teacher. You can enjoy life without abandoning yourself to sin and madness.

"Eat, drink, and be merry!—not with the attitude of the Epicureans, not because life is meaningless and nothing else matters, but realizing that food and wine and clothes and human love are all gifts from the hand of God. God is favoring you with these gifts *now,* so why foolishly wait until some future date?" (Ehlke, p. 96).

The Preacher has previously stated his alternate conclusion five times (2:24-26; 3:12, 13; 3:22; 5:18; 8:15). Here in verse 7-10 we have his most comprehensive and final presentation of the enjoy life advice. It recapitulates much of the earlier material. But it also adds three new elements:

1. Celebrative clothes and oil (verse 8)
2. Enjoy the love of one's spouse (verse 9)
3. An admonition to enthusiastic work (verse 10)

Although verses 7-10 with their call to enjoy life may represent a shift in mood from the somberness of verses 2-6, we still find continuity between the two passages. Even the enjoy life verses "contain repeated reminders of the emptiness and transience of human life" (Murphy and Huwiler, p. 209). Verse 9, for example, reminds us that our days are "fleeting" and verse 10 tells readers that they are heading for Sheol (the grave), where "there is no activity or planning or knowledge or wisdom." Thus the "commands to enjoy life" appear in the framework of "a steady reminder that this is not the ultimate solution to the question of meaning" (Longman, p. 230).

In Ecclesiastes 9:11, 12 the Preacher closes his fourth and final essay on the absurdity of life by exploring the problem of random chance. Here he again challenges traditional wisdom, which held that good conduct brings desirable results. Not so, the Preacher declares. The swiftest doesn't always win the race, the best warrior doesn't necessarily win the battle, nor do the discerning always end up with more wealth. Why? "Time and chance overtake them all" (verse 11). Beyond that, even the best of humans can fall on evil times, and we cannot predict if or when such catastrophes will happen (verse 12).

With such "happy" thoughts the Preacher brings to a close his extended and repeated demonstration of the meaninglessness of life. But remember, his entire discussion originates from an under the sun perspective. He himself will soar above the sun in his last chapter. But the fullest flight takes place in the New Testament.

If the dead for the Preacher have no hope (9:4), the life, death, and resurrection of Christ, whom God raised as the firstfruit of those who believe on Him, will reverse that fact. Because He conquered death His followers will also rise from it (1 Cor. 15:22, 23). Death and some form of hope are not only central to the message of the Preacher, but also to the apostle Paul. "But we would not have you ignorant, brethren, concerning those who are asleep, that you may not grieve as others do who have *no hope*. For since we believe that Jesus died and rose again, even so, through Jesus, God will bring with Him those who have fallen asleep. For this we declare to you by the word of the Lord, that we who are alive, who are left until the coming of the Lord, shall not precede those who have fallen asleep. For the Lord himself will descend from heaven with a cry of command, with the archangel's call, and with the sound of the trumpet of God. And the dead in Christ will rise first; then we who are alive, who are left, shall be caught up together with them in the clouds to meet the Lord in the air; and so we shall always be with the Lord. Therefore *comfort* one another with these words" (1 Thess. 4:13-18, RSV).

Now here is hope. Here is a view of the fullness of an above the sun revelation of the meaning of the death that comes to all.

17. Still More Words of Advice

Ecclesiastes 9:13–10:20

¹³Also this I came to see as wisdom under the sun, and it impressed me. ¹⁴There was a small city with few men in it and a great king came to it, surrounded it and constructed large siegeworks against it. ¹⁵But there was found in it a poor wise man and he delivered the city by his wisdom. Yet no one remembered that poor man. ¹⁶So I said, "Wisdom is better than strength." But the wisdom of the poor man is despised and his words are not heeded. ¹⁷The words of the wise heard in quietness are better than the shouting of a ruler among fools. ¹⁸Wisdom is better than weapons of war, but one sinner destroys much good.

10 *Dead flies make a perfumer's oil stink, so a little foolishness is weightier than wisdom and honor. ²A wise man's heart directs him toward the right, but the foolish man's heart directs him toward the left. ³Even when the fool walks along the road, his sense is lacking and he demonstrates to everyone that he is a fool. ⁴If the ruler's temper rises against you, do not abandon your position, because composure allays great offense.*

⁵There is an evil I have seen under the sun, like an error which goes forth from the ruler—⁶folly is set in many exalted places while rich men sit in humble places. ⁷I have seen slaves riding on horses and princes walking like slaves on the land.

⁸He who digs a pit may fall into it, and a serpent may bite him who breaks through a wall. ⁹He who quarries stones may be hurt by them, and he who splits logs may be endangered by them. ¹⁰If the axe is dull and he does not sharpen its edges, then he must exert more strength. Wisdom has the advantage of giving success. ¹¹If the serpent bites before being charmed, there is no profit for the charmer. ¹²Words from the mouth of a wise man are gracious, while the lips of a fool consume him; ¹³the beginning of his talking is folly and the end of it is wicked madness. [14]Yet the fool multiplies words. No man knows what will happen, and who can tell him what will come after him? [15]The toil of a fool so wearies him that he does not even know how to go to a city. [16]Woe to you, O land, whose king is a lad and whose princes feast in the morning. [17]Blessed are you, O land, whose king is of nobility and whose princes eat at the appropriate time—for strength and not drunkenness. [18]Through indolence the rafters sag, and through slackness the house leaks. [19]Men prepare a meal for enjoyment, and wine makes life merry, and money is the answer to everything. [20]Furthermore, in your bedchamber do not curse a king, and in your sleeping rooms do not curse a rich man, for a bird of the heavens will carry the sound and the winged creature will make the matter known.

A t last," writes Derek Kidner, "Qoheleth has finished his work of demolition. The site has been cleared: he can turn to building and planting" (Kidner, *Message*, p. 87). For nine chapters the Preacher has focused on demonstrating the absurdity of life under the sun (on earth). It is true that he offered short sections on good advice (4:9-12; 5:1-12; 7:1-8:9) and other passages on how to cope in what appears to be a meaningless existence (2:24-26; 3:12, 13, 22; 5:18-20; 8:15; 9:7-10), but his focus has been on tearing down. Now in his last three chapters he switches to building up. The bulk of those three chapters consists of what we termed "words of advice" in the outline to Ecclesiastes on page 25 and 26.

Extending from Ecclesiastes 9:13 to 12:7 this segment forms the longest section of the Preacher's book. It falls into three sections:

1. Proverbial guidelines for practical living (9:13-10:20)
2. Financial matters (11:1-8)
3. Capitalizing on the good things of life in our youth (11:9-12:7)

The present chapter treats the guidelines found in Ecclesiastes 9:13-10:20. David Hubbard suggests that the passage's "overall theme is the virtue and fragility of wisdom. In its contrasts of wise and foolish conduct in government and society it resembles the Book of Proverbs more than does any other section of Ecclesiastes" (Hubbard, *Ecclesiastes*, p. 208). In a general sort of way the material divides into six proverbial clusters.

The first cluster (9:13-18) centers on wisdom (verse 13). The Preacher begins with a four act word picture.

- The first act pictures a fragile little city that could muster only a few defenders (verse 14).
- By way of contrast, the second act tells us that a great king built siegeworks all around it (verse 14). Those siegeworks may have been elevated platforms from which the attackers could launch arrows and other projectiles over the walls of what was rapidly becoming an undefendable *little* city. Habbakuk 1:10 announces that "they [the Chaldeans] laugh at all fortified cities; they build earthen ramps and capture them" (NIV), giving us an idea of what threatened the besieged town. Things look dismal at best.
- But wonder of wonders! Act three presents "a poor wise man" who delivers the city by his wisdom (verse 15). What a blessing! A hero has arisen, saving the little city from the horrors of an invasion. We would expect everyone to honor him.
- Then comes the totally unexpected conclusion. Act four tells us that the city's inhabitants completely forget the poor wise man and ignore him during the victory celebration and thereafter (verse 15). The point the Preacher is making relates to the absolute importance of wisdom, but "how readily it can be shelved when the battle is over" (Hubbard, *Ecclesiastes*, p. 210).

The Preacher utilizes his four-act drama to highlight three crucial points about wisdom. First, "wisdom is better than strength" (verse 16), as demonstrated in the story. Second, quiet wisdom is better than blustering power (verse 17). And, third, as the tale illustrated, wisdom is more effective in the long run than lethal weapons (verse 18).

"But!" and there always seems to be a *but* in Ecclesiastes. *But* one stupid sinner can undo all that wisdom has accomplished *(ibid.)*.

That thought brings us to the second proverbial cluster (10:1-3), which takes folly or foolishness as its topic. Verse 1 picks up on 9:18's statement that "one sinner destroys much good," with its comparison of a small rotting fly spoiling a whole batch of valuable perfume to the influence of a fool outweighing the impact of honor and wisdom. Nobert Lohfink argues that in verse 1 we should translate the Hebrew to mean "stupid" rather than "foolish." "Up to now," he points out, "it was about a lack of education. It was something that could be remedied. It was not stupidity. Now we are shown a further flaw in the efficacy of the intellect: the limits of the intelligence" (Lohfink, p. 125).

Verses 2 and 3 illustrate the effects of stupidity. Such defective people not only take the wrong direction (verse 2), they can't even find their way to town on a well-marked road, thus demonstrating their incompetence to all (verse 3). Once again the Preacher has pushed home his point that for all of its faults wisdom (9:13-18) is better than folly or foolishness (10:1-3).

The third proverbial cluster (10:4-7) focuses on political authority. Verse 4 sets the stage with a foolish ruler who loses his temper. The way to relate to such a foolish person, the Preacher points out, is to remain calm, thereby keeping one's wisdom in control rather than allowing the passions to rule. Such a wise course often solves the problem. But Ecclesiastes has not finished with foolish rulers yet. The biblical writer tells us in verses 5-7 that they all too often appoint the wrong people to power. Uneducated slaves receive powerful positions that they are unprepared to handle in a wise manner, while those who have had the privileges of good training for wise leadership get left in humble and obscure positions. To the Preacher that is political stupidity. He doesn't explicitly suggest how to rectify the situation, but implicit in his argument is the idea that the way of wisdom is to put prepared people in the right places.

The next group of proverbs offers lessons related to work (verses 8-11). The saying that "wisdom has the advantage of giving success" (verse 10) provides the key for understanding the entire passage. Thus one must use wisdom in such work activities as digging a pit, remodeling a home, working with heavy stones, or splitting logs. To perform such activities carelessly (foolishly) is to risk danger (verses 8-10). Likewise, it is a stupid snake charmer indeed who employs his charming techniques after getting bitten (verse 11).

Group five (verses 12-15) in the proverbial lineup of Ecclesiastes 9:13-10:20 takes words as its major theme. For years I kept a little saying on my office wall. It was framed with a picture of a giraffe and pointed out that "it is better to remain silent and have people think you are stupid than to open your mouth and remove all doubt."

The wisdom writers of the Bible had a great deal to say about words and speech. We need only to think of the book of Proverbs, or James' teaching that one's tongue is like a small rudder that steers a great ship (3:4, 5), or of Jesus' insight that a person's words reveal their inner being (Matt.

12:34). The teaching on the use of words in Ecclesiastes 10:12-14 offers more counsel along the same line. For the Preacher, people's words are definitely an outward indicator as to whether they are wise or foolish.

> "It is better to remain silent and have people think you are stupid than to open your mouth and remove all doubt."

Verse 15 merely highlights what it means to be a fool. Not only are the words of such individuals senseless, but they cannot successfully accomplish the simplest tasks. The saying that they don't "even know how to get to a city" is somewhat equivalent to our saying "they can't even find their way home." (Ancient cities were built on hill tops or mounds and thus quite conspicuous.)

The final group of proverbs returns to the wisdom needed by rulers (verses 16-20). Verses 16 and 17 contrast the inadequate, foolish ruler with one who is wise and mature enough to know when and how to live a life of responsibility. The foolish play around ("feast in the morning"), while the wise have a sense of proportion that allows them to put their responsibilities before their personal pleasures. Verse 18 tells us that people, including rulers, "who sit around doing nothing will end up with a disaster on their hands" (Longman, p. 251). And verse 19, with its talk of food, wine, and money, reiterates the fact that wise people get their values straight—unlike the foolish and immature prince of verse 16 who thought life was for feasting and dissipation.

Harking back to verse 4 and Ecclesiastes 8:2-5, verses 19 and 20 offer counsel on the art of survival when dealing with rulers and other powerful people. Here the specific advice is that people need to be careful how they speak about individuals with authority since such words have a way of finding their way to their ears to the detriment of those who don't use discretion. Wise people are not gossips is one way of summing up the general principle undergirding the Preacher's point. Who amongst us hasn't been embarrassed from time to time when our words about others have gotten back to them?

Ecclesiastes 9:13-10:30, as we noted above, specializes in good advice. And that good advice should help those who ponder these verses and put them into practice so that they can better live the life of wisdom. To ignore such counsel is to follow the path of the fool. The Preacher knows that we are good at being foolish. But his advice, as he begins to more forcefully build toward his powerful conclusion, will help us avoid our natural inclinations. He wants you and me to escape the pits we are so talented at digging for ourselves (verse 8) and to enjoy a fuller life, even here under the sun.

18. Advice on Financial Topics

Ecclesiastes 11:1-8

> ¹*Cast your bread on the surface of the waters, for you will find it after many days. ²Divide your portion to seven, or even to eight, for you do not know what misfortune may occur on the earth. ³If the clouds are full, they pour out rain upon the earth; and whether a tree falls toward the south or toward the north, wherever the tree falls, there it lies. ⁴He who watches the wind will not sow and he who looks at the clouds will not reap. ⁵Just as you do not know the path of the wind and how bones are formed in the womb of the pregnant woman, so you do not know the activity of God who makes all things.*
>
> ⁶*Sow your seed in the morning and do not be idle in the evening, for you do not know whether morning or evening sowing will succeed, or whether both of them alike will be good.*
>
> ⁷*The light is pleasant, and it is good for the eyes to see the sun. ⁸Indeed, if a man should live many years, let him rejoice in them all, and let him remember the days of darkness, for they will be many. Everything that is to come will be futility.*

Wisdom, as the Preacher has agreed so far, is important in every area of life. Ecclesiastes 11:1-8 treats it in financial matters. In particular, the passage deals with the element of risk that resides in the commercial and agricultural realms, but notes that wise people must still move forward with their eyes open in spite of the dangers. The Preacher closes the passage by claiming that people need to take joy from life, all the while remembering that an individual's days of joy are limited by the certainty of death.

"Cast thy bread upon the waters: for thou shalt find it after many days" (verse 1, KJV). Interpretations of this and the following verse have centered upon two quite different themes. According to the first, the Preacher advises the giving of alms and assistance to a number of people ("seven or eight"—verse 2). Though you do not know how you will receive your reward, the exposition runs, it still will come. Michael Fox notes that "the 'giving' may include more than charitable donations." He quotes one Jewish source as saying, "'do a favor for a man from whom you never expect to benefit, because in the far future he will do a favor for you'" (Fox, *Ecclesiastes,* p. 72). That teaching was widespread in the ancient world. The Egyptian Instructions of Ankhsheshonqy, for example, advises its readers to "do a good deed and throw it in the water; when it dries up you will find it" (19:10, quoted in Crenshaw, *Education,* p. 79). The charitable interpretation was also predominant in the early Christian church (see J. R. Wright, pp. 273, 274).

A modern scholar who takes the chartable approach cautions that we need to beware that we do not be generous just so that we may reap a reward, because such an attitude is "against the spirit of true generosity." Yet, he points out, even though generous people are not looking for a reward, "sometimes in unexpected ways, a reward comes" (Davidson, p. 78).

> ## The "Law" of Generosity
>
> "It is generous people, people who spend their lives giving of themselves to others, who find that, when they are in need, they have a host of friends. It is selfish people, who close their hearts to others, who end up finding that they may have plenty of this world's goods but no real friends" (Davidson, p. 78).

Whereas the majority of ancient Jewish and Christian commentators held the charitable interpretation, most modern students of Ecclesiastes see the text in terms of wise counsel applying to commercial investment. Thus James Crenshaw writes of casting one's bread upon the waters that "this strange advice seems to relate to maritime commercial ventures; Qohelet urges the taking of risks, the sending forth to distant ports in the hope of obtaining a substantial profit. One should be willing to take risks, confident that surprising results may follow" (Crenshaw, *Ecclesiastes,* p. 178).

In such enterprises the "after many days" was quite realistic. A delay often transpired before any profit resulted. For example, Solomon's fleet returned every three years bringing its exotic and valuable cargo of "gold and silver, ivory and apes and peacocks" (1 Kings 10:22).

Many modern commentators choose not to overly restrict the type of commercial enterprises being discussed in verse 1 to shipping, but see it as wise advice on investments in general.

The interpretation of verse 2 depends upon that of verse 1. Those who take the charitable approach see the counsel to "divide your portion to seven, or even to eight, for you do not know what misfortune may occur on the earth?" to infer that if a person is kind to a large number of people, some of them may be around to help if hard times fall on him or her.

Alternatively, others see the counsel in relation to diversification of investments. After all, if pirates attack one ship or it gets destroyed in a storm, others will still return to port with a profit. In modern terms the counsel of verse 2 would be to diversify investment portfolios. One gets the impression that if the Preacher lived in our day he would advise mutual funds that provide a good balance between stocks and bonds.

Verse 3, with its talk of full clouds pouring out rain appears to be urging the wisdom of close observation so that we can properly time our expenditures of time and money. After all, the fabric of reality has certain natural laws woven into it. Some things happen without regard to human effort. Thus when clouds are full they empty themselves. We cannot change such facts of life. But we can work in harmony with them. So let's get on with our work, our wisdom being informed by intelligent observation.

Some, unfortunately, spend all their time observing, waiting for the perfect time, and never quite get around to the "casting" or work. Such seems to be the problem of those in verse 4, who watch the wind and clouds, waiting for the most opportune moment to sow and harvest. But one never knows when the wind will not scatter the seeds or when the rain will not destroy any of the harvest. They wait for the ideal time, but it never comes. Their perfectionism stymies their action and it inevitably results in loss. Such is the plague of perfectionism in every area of life. The Preacher knows that successful living is a calculated risk. It is important that we observe, but it is equally important that we move forward when we have a good (though not perfect) probability for success.

We need to face the fact that there exist lots of things we just don't

know. He lists three of our don't knows in verse 5:
1. Where the wind comes from,
2. how bones are formed in an expectant mother, and
3. how God works.

And those three are just the tip of our ignorance iceberg. Humble up my friend. If you are waiting for perfect knowledge before you invest your time and energy, you will never do anything.

The Preacher's punch line is in verse 6, in which he tells us to sow both in the morning and the evening (all the time), since we don't know when our efforts will bear fruit.

Robert Davidson sums up the teaching of Ecclesiastes 11:1-6 nicely when he writes that "if we are going to wait until we are absolutely sure as to what God wants us to do and exactly when he wants us to do it, we are going to wait for a long time. . . . Get cracking, redouble your efforts: you cannot guarantee results, but you increase your chances if you are diligent and make the most of the chances that come your way. There is nothing more sad than looking back on life and seeing it as a series of missed opportunities and thinking, 'If only I had done that!' Do what you have to do, do what you can do—now" (Davidson, p. 80).

And after you've done it, don't be backward about enjoying it. "The light is pleasant, and it is good for the eyes to see the sun. Indeed, if a man should live many years, let him rejoice in them all" (verses 7, 8a). It is not a sin to enjoy the fruits of our labor or investment or casting (verse 1) or sowing (verse 6). After all, the Preacher has repeatedly told us that the simple enjoyments of life come from God, and He expects us to take pleasure in them (2:24; 3:13; 5:18).

But while you are finding pleasure in what you have accomplished, remember that it is not an end in itself, that living for things and pleasures is nothing short of meaninglessness (2:1-11). The Preacher has driven that point home repeatedly. The wise person puts everything in perspective and remembers that the days of darkness and death will come and will transform everything into "futility" (verse 8b). The biblical author will pick up on the darkness theme in Ecclesiastes 11:9-12:8 and elaborate it to its fullness in an attempt to enable his readers to develop a true perspective of earthly (under the sun) existence.

Meanwhile, Jesus will more fully develop the theme of Ecclesiastes

11:1-6 in His parable of the talents (Matt. 25:14-30). "Part of our commitment to Jesus as Lord is our commitment to invest our money, our time, our energy in endeavors that will pay dividends" (Hubbard, *Beyond Futility,* pp. 115, 116).

19. Advice to Young People

Ecclesiastes 11:9–12:8

⁹*Rejoice, young man, during your childhood, and let your heart be pleasant during the days of young manhood. And follow the impulses of your heart and the desires of your eyes. Yet know that God will bring you to judgment for all these things.* ¹⁰*So, remove grief and anger from your heart and put away pain from your body, because childhood and the prime of life are fleeting.*

12¹*Remember also your Creator in the days of your youth, before the evil days come and the years draw near when you will say, "I have no delight in them";* ²*before the sun and the light, the moon and the stars are darkened, and clouds return after the rain;* ³*in the day that the watchmen of the house tremble, and mighty men stoop, the grinding ones stand idle because they are few, and those who look through windows grow dim;* ⁴*and the doors of the street are shut as the sound of the grinding mill is low, and one will arise at the sound of the bird and all the daughters of song will sing softly.* ⁵*Furthermore, men are afraid of a high place and of terrors on the road; the almond tree blossoms, the grasshopper drags himself along, and the caperberry is ineffective. For man goes to his eternal home while mourners go about in the street.* ⁶*Remember Him before the silver cord is broken and the golden bowl is crushed, the pitcher by the well is shattered and the wheel at the cistern is crushed;* ⁷*then the dust will return to the earth as it was, and the spirit [breath] will return to God who gave it.* ⁸*"Vanity of vanities," says the Preacher, "all is vanity!"*

How to live life? And why live it that particular way? are questions that face every person. Those of us who are older have come to grips with them in one way or another. But they are still open questions for the young.

The Preacher addresses his last segment of advice to the needs of the young, and it is a finely crafted piece of instruction that carefully balances the how to live with the reasons one should live that way—that is, instruction and motivation.

Verse 9 utilizes both sides of the balance. On the one hand, we find instruction worded in such a way that it is a command. "Rejoice, young man, during your childhood, and let you heart be pleasant during the days of young manhood. And follow the impulses of your heart and the desires of your eyes." That instruction is not a new concept in Ecclesiastes. We have repeatedly found it throughout the book as he counseled people to enjoy life in spite of its frustrations and seeming meaninglessness (2:24-26; 3:12, 13, 22; 5:18-20; 8:15; 9:7-10).

"Yet," the Preacher forcefully adds, "know that God will bring you to judgment for all these things." Here we find the motivational aspect.

Some have concluded that enjoying life and the ever present thought of judgment don't fit together. Scholars have even argued that while the enjoy command came from the Preacher, a second writer who feared that the pleasure and the fulfilling of desires might get out of hand then added the warning of judgment.

But, as Ellen Davis points out, the two halves of verse 9 do go together. "The complementarity," she writes, "has two aspects. First, the mention of judgment clarifies the nature of proper enjoyment. It is *responsible* pleasure, not license to exploit others or squander our own bodies and abilities. Such pleasure bespeaks genuine responsiveness to what God has given us. . . .

"The second aspect of complementarity" focuses on the fact that "judgment does not cancel out rejoicing but on the contrary makes it imperative. Could it be that this is the chief thing for which we have to answer to God (see Phil. 4:4-5 [in which Paul commands us to rejoice])? Koheleth's repeated observation that 'there is nothing better for people under the sun than to . . . enjoy themselves' (3:12; 8:15) is not a counsel of despair but a call to responsibility before the God who is continually *taking us into account,* which is what God's judgment is. Our enjoyment is the right answer to God's abiding . . . interest in the creatures who bear something like a family resemblance to God. Is not the children's joy the answer that the parent's love most desires?" (Davis, pp. 222, 223).

Another way of expressing such logic is to say that those who do not accept and enjoy the good things that God has provided them as Creator are in fact rejecting Him. With that thought we come to the foundation of a Christian theology of aesthetics. When God created the world He declared it good. That goodness includes our appetites (including the sexual) and those aspects of creation that God so carefully crafted to satisfy them. Only sick people (and sick church members) desire to spurn God's good gifts. And that rejection is a part of what judgment is all about. The last thing God wants in heaven for the ceaseless ages of eternity is a group of straight-faced zombies, who frown at everything God has provided. Enjoying life begins on this earth. As Ellen White so nicely put it, "What we now are . . . is the sure foreshadowing of what we shall be" (White, *Education*, p. 307). Thus the Preacher's command to begin rejoicing in the days of our youth.

Whereas verse 9 advises pleasure, verse 10 counsels the removal of displeasures, including grief, anger, and pain. Such problems are usually the stuff of old age. Young people will be old soon enough since "childhood and the prime of life are fleeting." It is a needless waste for youth to act like old men and old women. Theirs is the time for rejoicing.

The command to "remember also your Creator in the days of your youth" (verse 1) ties chapter 11 to Ecclesiastes 12:1-7. It summons us to look beyond ourselves, to remember that we are not the center of the universe. We must do away with egocentricity and keep in mind that we are not self-sufficient, that it is God who has created both our bodies and those things that bring us joy and pleasure.

> **Joy and Judgment**
> Verse 9, "by insisting that our ways matter to God and are therefore meaningful through and through, robs joy of nothing but its hollowness. . . . Joy was created to dance with goodness, not alone" (Kidner, *Message*, pp. 99, 100).

But verse 1 is also a warning that the exuberant, carefree, joyous days of youth will not go on forever. In chapter 3 the Preacher told us that there is a time for everything, including a time to die, and that there is nothing that fragile humans can do to stem the ongoing flow of time (verses 2, 14). So it is that "the evil days" will come and the years will draw near "when you will say, 'I have no delight in them'" (12:1).

Ecclesiastes 12:1-7 is one of the more well known sections of the book. Michael Fox notes that it "is a powerful poem, even if we don't quite know what it means." "Actually," he adds, "we do know what it means: enjoy life before you grow old and die. What we don't know is how it means it. [But] the poem retains its power even over those who do not understand it completely" (Fox, *A Time to Tear Down*, p. 333).

Some interpret verses 2-7 as reflecting on the gradual deterioration of the body that ends up in death. Others see the passage as presenting a funeral procession. Arguments can be made for both interpretations, and neither of them satisfactorily explain all the details. But the good news is that we don't need to understand all of them. No matter how we interpret the bits and pieces, Ecclesiastes 12:2-7 "remains one of the most powerful evocations of death ever written" (Davis, p. 225).

As I see it, these six verses present three memorable word pictures of an aging body arriving at death. The first compares aging to the coming of winter. The chill of winter pervades verse 2, as the days darken and the rains begin to arrive. The rains, the verse notes, not only come, but they keep on pouring down. Whereas in happier seasons one can expect clearing after a storm, in the depth of winter the "clouds return after the rain." Rain follows rain.

So it is in aging. "In one's early years, and for the greater part of life, troubles and illnesses are chiefly setbacks, not disasters. One expects the sky to clear eventually. . . . Now, in the final stretch, there will be no improvement: the clouds will always gather again, and time will no longer heal, but kill" (Kidner, *Message*, p. 102).

The second word picture symbolizes the body as a deteriorating house, with the once strong members becoming enfeebled, the number of teeth (grinders) dwindling, the eyes (windows) growing dimmer (verse 3), the ears losing their effectiveness, and sleep becoming so light that the sound of a bird is enough to awaken one (verse 4). Beyond that, with their sense of balance deteriorating the elderly become afraid of high places and they tend increasingly to fear the unknown. Their hair turns white like the blossom of an almond tree, and they kind of creep around like an aging grasshopper who no longer bounds from place to place. And lastly, "the caperberry is ineffective" (verse 5). The ancients regarded the caperberry (the green bud or berry of the mediterranean shrub *capparis sicula*) as a stimulant to the appetites, including sexual desire. The Revised Standard Version is to the point when it says "desire fails." But the Jewish paraphrase on the passage in Aramaic is even more graphic: "You will cease from sexual intercourse" (cited in Garrett, p. 342).

People may differ on how to interpret the details of Ecclesiastes 12:2-5, but those who have advanced sufficiently through the aging process get the picture. Perhaps the best biblical illustration is the reply of the elderly Barzillai to David's offer of a place at court: "I am this day eighty years old; can I discern what is pleasant and what is not? Can your servant taste what he eats or what he drinks? Can I still listen to the voice of singing men and singing women?" (2 Sam. 19:35, RSV). And then of course we have the case of the aged Abraham who had to take it on faith that he could have a son because he knew that "his own body" was "as good as dead" (Rom. 4:19).

The last part of Ecclesiastes 12:5 points to the final end of a deteriorating body when it claims that people go to their "eternal home." In this context "eternal home" means grave rather than heavenly dwelling place. The thought of death brings us to verse 6 and the final word picture. It is one not of the decaying body but of death itself. The author compares the transition from life to death to the snapping of a thread and the crushing of a bowl.

Verse 7 describes what takes place at death. The body (dust) goes back to the earth and the breath (spirit) "will return to God who gave it." The Hebrew *ruah* can be translated as either "spirit" or "breath" (see Botterweck, vol. XIII, pp. 375, 386; Harris, vol. II, p. 836). We know that the translation in Ecclesiastes 12:7 should be "breath" because the verse is an exact reversal of Genesis 2:7, in which God created humans: "Then the Lord God formed man of dust from the ground, and breathed into his nostrils the *breath* of life; and man became a living being." According to the Preacher death is merely the reversal of the creation process. Thus at death the body decays in the grave and the life-giving breath returns to God. As a result, O. S. Rankin is correct when he asserts that in verse 7 "Koheleth does not mean that man's personality continues to exist" (Rankin, p. 86; cf. p. 52).

For the Preacher there is no more to say. Death has come. But wait, he does have one final word. "Vanity of vanities, . . . all is vanity!" (12:8). And with that he has made the full circle. He began his book with the same statement (1:2). This repetition envelopes the body of the book of

Ecclesiastes. In between he has demonstrated repeatedly that life under the sun is absurd in itself (1:4-2:26; 3:1-4:16; 5:13-6:12; 8:10-9:12). When it comes right down to it, the Preacher, after all his investigations, is just as baffled about life from an under the sun perspective as when he began his quest: "all is vanity" or absurdity or meaninglessness.

Even Ecclesiastes 12:8, though, is not the final word on ultimate meaning. The book's final two verses (12:13, 14) transcend meaninglessness by leading readers to an "above the sun" conclusion.

But before turning to Ecclesiastes' concluding verses we need to reiterate the fact that Jesus and the apostles specialize in above the sun revelations of the true significance of life. Beyond that, they help us clearly see that the grave that so much disturbed the Preacher in his under the sun mode is not the end, but rather a stopping or resting place on the way to resurrection and immortality, which take place at the second advent of Christ (1 Cor. 15:51-55; 1 Thess. 4:13-18; John 14:1-3).

Part III

Meaninglessness Transcended

Ecclesiastes 12:9–14

20. There Is Meaning After All

Ecclesiastes 12:9-14

[9] *In addition to being a wise man, the Preacher also taught the people knowledge; and he pondered, searched out and arranged many proverbs.* [10] *The Preacher sought to find delightful words and to write words of truth correctly.*

[11] *The words of wise men are like goads, and masters of these collections are like well-driven nails; they are given by one Shepherd.* [12] *But beyond this, my son, be warned: the writing of many books is endless, and excessive devotion to books is wearying to the body.*

[13] *The conclusion, when all has been heard, is: fear God and keep His commandments, because this applies to every person.* [14] *For God will bring every act to judgment, everything which is hidden, whether it is good or evil.*

Who wrote these final verses?

The question needs to be asked, since the text of Ecclesiastes has shifted from the first person ("I saw") to the third ("the Preacher . . . taught"). That is, these verses talk about the Preacher rather than presenting what he personally saw and concluded. We found the same approach in the book's opening verses (1:1, 2). That fact has led some to argue that an editor framed the words of the Preacher (1:3-12:8) with an introduction (1:1, 2) and a conclusion (12:9-14). Still other students of the book hold for two editors, with the first framing the words of the Preacher in Ecclesiastes 1:1, 2 and 12:9-12 and the second, worried about the wrong conclusions that readers might draw from the book, adding the final two verses dealing with fearing God, keeping the commandments, and judgment in an attempt to make Ecclesiastes and its author look more orthodox (see Loader, pp. 133-136).

But such speculations are not necessary. As Ellen Davis points out, "the themes of fearing God and God's judgment have been introduced numerous times by Koheleth himself" (Davis, p. 226). Beyond that, literature offers many examples of authors standing back and discussing their own works in the third person. Thus we have no compelling reason for seeing more than one author or editor for the book of Ecclesiastes.

While it is true that the certainty of Ecclesiastes 12:13, 14 seems to stand in contrast with the more tentative body of the book, it appears that the best explanation for the difference occurs in the book itself. The bulk of Ecclesiastes represents an exploration of meaning from an under the sun perspective. But in its final verses the author presents an unqualified above the sun viewpoint on the meaning of life and human duty. The Preacher may have framed his book with the observation that everything under the sun is absurd (1:2, 3; 12:8), but it is significant that it is not his final conclusion. He declares from an above the sun perspective that the "whole duty of man" is to "fear God, and keep his commandments. . . . For God will bring every deed into judgment" (12:13, 14, RSV). That, H. C. Leupold notes, is "the author's own statement of the theme of his book" (Leupold, p. 299). Thus the fact is that everything under the sun is vanity is not the major theme of the Preacher. Rather, that assertion is the evangelistic pointer to the need for an above the sun solution in the book's final verses, which transcend the motif of the bulk of Ecclesiastes.

Beginning in Ecclesiastes 12:9 the author stands back and provides us with a three-verse analysis of his ministry. In verse 9 he tells us he is a "wise man." Some have claimed that if the Preacher actually called himself a wise man we could fault him for bragging. To the contrary. He used it as a designation of social location. As Walter Kaiser notes, "the term 'wise' marked him as a member of one of the three great institutions of his day: prophet, priest, and wise man (cf. Jer. 8:8-9; 18:18; Ezek. 7:26). The designation was a technical one, marking him as a member of the wise to whom God gave wisdom, just as the priest had the Law and the prophet had the Word" (Kaiser, p. 123).

The Preacher not only "taught the people knowledge," but he had a literary life in which he aggressively collected ("searched out"), thought deeply about ("pondered"), and "arranged" or composed "many proverbs." For most of recorded history proverbs have served as a major tool for transmitting knowledge from one generation to the next. We have written records that human beings have summarized lessons from life experience all the way back to ancient Samaria and Egypt. Thus the Preacher as a creator of proverbs was in good company not only within Israel but in the surrounding nations. Most of them had collections of proverbial wisdom that often overlapped in content since proverbs by and large represent summaries of commonsense observations as to what worked and failed in everyday life.

The Preacher not only composed proverbs but tells us that he sought the most pleasing and accurate words (12:10). The carefully crafted book of Ecclesiastes is a witness to the success of his methodology.

Few passages in the Bible are more explicit about the literary method of an inspired writer. "Incidentally," Leupold points out, "we catch one of the few glimpses behind the scenes in the process of . . . inspiration" as God used human beings (see comments on verse 11) to produce the written Word of God (Leupold, p. 294).

Ecclesiastes 12:11 sets forth the function of wisdom literature. "The sayings of the wise are like goads, and like nails firmly fixed are the collected sayings which are given by one Shepherd" (RSV). Here the Preacher tells us three things about his writings. One concerns their source: the "one Shepherd," a reference to God, whom Scripture refers to by that title in such places as Psalms 80:1 and 23:1. The other two deal with function. His writings were to act as a goad, a sharp, pointed stake used to prod an animal to get it to go in the right direction. They were also to act as nails, a device used to hold something firmly in place. Thus the writings of the wise give direction to people's lives and help their memories retain important information. With those goals in mind, it is no wonder that the Preacher searched to find the most pleasing and correct words in which to pass on his message (12:10).

With Ecclesiastes 12:12-14 the focal point shifts from the duties of the Preacher to the responsibilities of his students, which includes you and me. The intent of verse 12 with its saying about many books is that human beings have written a great deal that is erroneous. Thus his warning. Such study not only fails to enlighten, but it ends up tiring people out. Certainly not all the thoughts coming from the sages in Israel were helpful (see Jer. 8:9). And beyond problematic Jewish writings were the sayings of the pagan thought leaders in the surrounding nations that often led Israel astray and were certainly not the product of the "one Shepherd" (see Eaton, p. 155).

Ecclesiastes ends in a thundering statement, as we noted above, that sets forth the Preacher's major thesis: "The end of the matter; all has been heard. Fear God, and keep his commandments; for this is the whole duty of man. For God will bring every deed into judgment, with every secret thing, whether good or evil" (12:13, 14, RSV).

The two mighty imperatives of verse 13 are

- "Fear God" and
- "keep His commandments."

Fearing God, as we noted earlier, is to respect and honor who He is. It is to put Him at the center of our lives. That command has echoed throughout the book (3:14; 5:7; 7:18; 8:13), but now it explicitly takes center stage.

The sequence of the two imperatives ("fear" and "keep") is absolutely crucial. After all, "conduct derives from worship. A knowledge of God leads to obedience; not vice versa" (Eaton, p. 156). It is the proper order that keeps God's people from the pit of legalism, of attempting to trade obedience for God's divine favor.

The keeping of God's commands includes all of what He has revealed and should not be limited to the Decalogue. It refers to all that we know of God's will. And it certainly includes the good advice and the injunctions to enjoy life that the Preacher scattered throughout his book. "Keeping God's commandments," Davis observes, "is an intelligent and faithful response to the cardinal fact that 'all is *hevel*' [vanity or absurdity or meaninglessness] (1:2; 12:8). For the one stable thing 'under the sun' is the revelation of God's will for our world. Therefore orienting our lives toward the commandments enables us, 'while we are placed among things that are passing away, to hold fast to those that shall endure'" (Davis, p. 228).

Obeying God, however, must never be a mere surface or outward matter, a truth implied by the fact that the judgment of Ecclesiastes 12:14 takes into account even the hidden things in our hearts and mind. In later times Jesus would make it explicitly clear that obedience must be from the heart. The Preacher was well aware of that truth.

The reference to divine judgment in the Preacher's conclusion is not something new. He previously alluded to it in Ecclesiastes 3:17 and 11:9.

But in 12:14 the author alerts us to its depth when he tells us that it will include not merely the good and evil aspects of life but "everything which is hidden." We can hide nothing from God. To attempt to do so, the Preacher might say, would be *hebel*, vanity, absurdity, foolishness. The Preacher does not tell us about the how or when of the judgment. He merely asserts its certainty. James Crenshaw notes that divine judgment is a "comforting word for good people" but a "frightening word for sinners" (Crenshaw, *Ecclesiastes*, p. 192). When it comes right down to the end the Preacher leaves his readers with an existential choice: either to live a life of fearing God and obeying his commands or to experience a life of vanity or meaninglessness. The biblical author knows of no third option.

We have reached the end of the book of Ecclesiastes, but we have not come to the end of its message. Instead, we find that it is a vital word of God right up to the close of time, a truth reflected in Revelation 14, which describes the messages of three angels to be proclaimed just before the Second Advent (verses 14-20). "Then," we read, "I saw another angel flying in midheaven, with an eternal gospel to proclaim to those who dwell on earth, to every nation and tribe and tongue and people; and he said with a loud voice, '*Fear God* and give him glory, for the hour of his *judgment* has come; and worship him who made heaven and earth, the sea and the fountains of water" (verses 6, 7, RSV). In addition to that message, the third angel of Revelation 14 helps us see that obedience to God's commandments will be an issue until the end of time (Rev. 14:12; cf. 12:17).

Thus in three short verses from the Apocalypse of John we find several echoes from the Preacher:

1. Fearing God (Eccl. 12:13).
2. Keeping His commandments (verse 13).
3. Remembering the Creator (verse 1), which is tied to God's commandments in Exodus 20:8-11 and Genesis 2:1-3.

When it comes right down to it, the book of Ecclesiastes is much more relevant to our day than most people recognize. It not only addresses the existential questioning of the twenty-first century mind, but it also concludes with a message that the Revelator tells us will be of great importance immediately before the Second Advent.

Exploring the
Song of
Solomon

Introduction to
the Song of Solomon

How did the Song of Solomon get into the Bible? Ecclesiastes with all of its questioning and doubt is bad enough. But that looks like a minor problem next to the explicitly sexual content of the Song. In addition, the book does not explicitly mention God even once. But it is worse than that. As G. Lloyd Carr points out, *"all* the major religious words in the Old Testament vocabulary" are missing (Carr, p. 43). Thus, for example, "Temple," "sanctuary," "congregation," "offering," "sacrifice," "blood," "priest," "atone," "faithful," "truth," "covenant," "bless," "sin," "wisdom," "grace," "mercy," "love," "be clean," "glory," "commandment," "justice," "save," "vow," "prophet," "righteousness," "holy," "spirit," "evil," "wickedness," "Sabbath," "worship," "bless," "heaven," "judgment," "law," and many other religious terms never appear in the Song.

"What kind of a book is this?" is the natural question to ask. Is it secular in intent or religious? Such concerns are not new. The Song and its place in Scripture have challenged both Jews and Christians throughout history.

The plain fact is that not all books had an equally smooth ride into the canon of the Bible. The Song of Solomon was one of those resisted by some. In the face of such disputes, Rabbi Akiba (cir. A.D. 50-132, the father of rabbinical Judaism) not only declared it to be an inspired book, but went on to say that "the entire age is not so worthy as the day on which the Song of Songs was given to Israel. For all the scriptures are holy, but the Song of Songs is holiest of all" (*Mishnah,* Yadayim 3:5).

Needless to say, it was because of its content not in spite of it that the Song became a part of the Jewish and later the Christian canon of inspired books. The issue of the sacred versus the secular did not disturb Hebrew thinking. The "idea of God permeating every area of life was fundamental to Israelite society. . . . So if we ask the question, 'Where is God in the Song?', the answer is 'Nowhere and everywhere.' He is nowhere explicitly mentioned, and everywhere assumed" (Gledhill, pp. 36, 37). This is His earth. He not only created the world but humans as male and female (Gen. 1:26, 27; 2:18-23). And it was He who instituted the state of marriage (2:24). From that perspective a book of poems celebrating the love of a man and a woman has a rightful place in the Bible.

The Jews divided the Hebrew Bible into the law, the prophets, and the writings. The Song is a part of the writings, one of five scrolls (Megilloth) which also included Ruth, Lamentations, Ecclesiastes, and Esther. Each was annually read on a Jewish holiday, with the Song's turn coming at Passover each spring.

Old Testament scholars disagree as to whether the Song should be included with Proverbs, Job, and Ecclesiastes as a part of the Bible's wisdom literature (see the introduction to Ecclesiastes for a discussion of wisdom literature). Strictly speaking, we should not classify it as wisdom literature, "since its dominant form is love poetry, not instruction or debate." But because of its connection with Solomon and the fact that the wisdom sages probably preserved and handed it down, commentators often include it in the category of wisdom literature (see La Sor, p. 603; Murphy, *Tree of Life*, pp. 106, 107).

From that perspective some have suggested that

- Job explores the riddle of suffering,
- Ecclesiastes explores the riddle of existence, and
- the Song explores the riddle of love.

Most English translations title the Song as the Song of Solomon, but the Hebrew text labels it the Song of Songs (1:1), that is, the best of songs much as king of kings means the supreme king or vanity of vanities refers to the most vain. The book is also known as Canticles, from the Latin Vulgate's title of *Canticum Canticorum.*

Interpretation of the Song

"No book in the Bible," Robert Davidson writes, "has been subject to more varied assessments as to its worth, or as to how we ought to understand it" (Robert Davidson, p. 93). Part of the difficulty comes from its often obscure poetic format and part from the fact that its explicit discussion of sexual intimacy makes a lot of people uncomfortable.

That uneasiness started with the ancient Jews. One of the earliest records we have of the book's interpretation comes from Rabbi Akiba, who about A.D. 100 remarked that "whoever sings the Song of Songs with tremulous voice in a banquet hall and (so) treats it as a sort of ditty . . . has no share in the world to come" (quoted in Murphy, *Song,* p. 13).

While, as the above quotation indicates, some made coarse use of the Song, others found themselves put off by that same sexuality. The solution for those in the latter camp was to allegorize the Song, thereby transforming it into a poem dealing with God's love for Israel.

The early Christian church also took up the allegorical approach. The fact that the early church was heavily influenced by Greek philosophic thought that held that body and soul are separate entities, with the body being a repository for the soul, also had a powerful role in moving interpretation away from the literal to the allegorical. In Neoplatonic thought "the body needed to be subjugated and eventually eliminated in death" (Longman, p. 30). With that view in mind, the Song obviously could not refer to physical pleasure. It must symbolize Christ's love for the church.

Especially influential along this line of thinking was Origen (A.D. 185-253/254), whose views on sexuality led him to castrate himself (Eusebius, *History* 6:8:5). Given his strong views, he also "desexed" the Song (Longman, p. 29). He tends to spend little time on the sexual level, noting that "these things seem to me to afford no profit to the reader as far as the story goes; nor do they maintain any continuous narrative such as we find in other Scripture stories. It is necessary, therefore, rather to give them all a spiritual meaning" (quoted in Murphy, *Song,* pp. 18, 19). So went his 10-volume commentary on the Song.

At one point Origen advised "everyone who is not yet rid of the vexations of the flesh and blood and has not ceased to feel the passions of this bodily nature, to refrain from reading the book and the things that will be said about it" (quoted in Gledhill, p. 30).

Jerome (cir. 347-420), translator of the Latin Vulgate Bible, popularized Origen's allegorical approach in the Western Church. A proponent of the ascetic lifestyle, he reportedly threw himself into thornbushes when as a youth he felt the beginning of sexual arousal. Since that didn't always help, he also immersed himself in the study of Hebrew to calm his desires (see Longman, p. 31).

Such were the views on sexuality that not only led the medieval church down the path stipulating that virginity and celibacy were the holiest ways to live but which also fueled the ongoing allegorical interpretation of the Song. Thus for more than a millennium "celibate Christian theologians were . . . able by allegory to unsex the Sublime Song and make it a hymn of spiritual and mystical love without carnal taint. *Canticum Canticorum* thus became the favorite book of ascetics and monastics who found in it, and in expansive sermons and commentaries on it, the means to rise above earthly and fleshly desire to the pure platonic love of the virgin soul for God. In the medieval cloisters . . . no other book of sacred Scripture received more attention than the Song of Songs" (Pope, p. 114).

The aversion to sexual matters didn't suddenly die with the coming of the Reformation and modernity. The generally quite earthy Martin Luther, for example, wrote that "the reproduction of mankind is a great marvel and mystery. Had God consulted me in the matter, I should have advised him to continue the generation of the species by fashioning them out of clay" (quoted in Gledhill, p. 171). And Lady Hillingdon, an aristocratic English woman of the Victorian era (late nineteen century), expressed her aversion to her husband's attentions in these words: "I am happy now that Charles calls on my bedchamber less frequently than of old. As it is, I now endure but two calls a week, and when I hear his steps outside my door, I lie down on my bed, close my eyes, . . . and think of England" until it is over *(ibid.)*.

It was such views of sex that fueled and continue to fuel in the twenty-first century the allegorical interpretation of the Song that views its symbolism as applying to Christ's love for the church. But, we should note, we do not find one hint in the Song itself that we should interpret it that way. Such approaches tell us more about the minds and fears of the commentators than they do about the Song itself, which suggests nothing but a literal sexual meaning.

Beyond the lack of authorization in the Song itself, the allegorical method has no interpretive stability, since each person applies different symbolic meaning to the text. Thus commentators do not allow the biblical text to control its own interpretation, and meaning tends to be read into it rather than out of it. The result is widely differing allegorical interpretations. Othmar Keel is quite on target when he observes that "if two allegorizers ever agree on the interpretation of a verse it is only because one has copied from the other" (Keel, p. 8).

The major alternative to the allegorical approach is a literal reading of the text for what it says. Thus when the Greek version of the Song says "let him kiss me with the kisses of his mouth: for thy breasts are better than wine" (1:2, LXX), we can translate the verse in terms of real kisses and real breasts rather than "justice and peace" kissing (Jerome) and "the breasts of law and grace, soothing our sorrows by telling of heavenly things" (Ambrose, cir. 333-397; both quoted in Wright, p. 291). The literal interpretation, one suggested by the text itself, views the Song as a series of poems between lovers.

An Important Interpretive Key

Before moving away from interpretive issues, we need to highlight the fact that the Song is a part of Scripture and is meant to be read in the context of the rest of God's word. Thus we should not approach the narrative from the perspective of the anti-physical philosophy of the Greeks, but rather in the context in which God created human bodies and marriage and declared them "good" (Gen. 1, 2). Again, rather than projecting into the text loose ideas of sex, the Song is to be read in the context of the law of God and the concept of marriage set forth in Genesis 2:24 (cf. Matt. 19:5).

"Within the biblical context," Richard Hess points out, "this positive theme of physical love contrasts strongly with the persistent negative statements on adultery, promiscuity, and the images of Israel as an unfaithful wife as found in the prophets." "The repeated appearance of 'bride' in the Song's heart (six times in 4:8-5:1) demonstrates a relationship that is one of marriage. . . . The language of commitment pervades the whole Song and provides one of the most important interpretive keys for understanding the work" (Hess, pp. 33, 28).

Purpose of the Song

It would be wrong to say that the Song was written to counteract the nonbiblical views of sex exhibited in the medieval, Victorian, and modern worlds, since they obviously came after the composition of the Song itself. But that is not a bad answer.

The Song is the one book in the Bible that makes its special focus human love and sexuality. As love poetry the Song has an important place in the Bible. "Imagine," urges Tremper Longman, "a Bible without the Song. Without the Song, the Church and synagogue would be left with spare and virtually exclusively negative words about an important aspect of our lives. Sexuality is a major aspect of the human experience, and God in his wisdom has spoken through the poet(s) of the Song to encourage us as well as warn us about its power in our lives" (Longman, p. 59).

In another place he comments that "the Song of Songs is a passionate, sensuous love poem that reminds us that God is interested in more than just our brains and our spirits; he wants us to enjoy our bodies" (in Hess, p. 8). That insight harmonizes with the repeated command in Ecclesiastes to eat, drink, and enjoy life (2:24-26; 3:12, 13, 22; 5:18-20; 8:15; 9:7-10), especially "with the woman whom you love" (9:9). The Song's love poetry reminds us that "we are not merely a soul encased in a body but whole persons made in God's image" (Longman in Hess, p. 8). The Song is the place in the Bible that God alerts us both to our sexuality and its complexity.

Its word pictures also help us keep in mind how important the affective and sexual part of our existence is. In answer to the question of why the Song is in the Bible, Edward Young writes that God placed it in the canon "in order to teach us the purity and sanctity of that estate of marriage which He Himself established" (Young, p. 355).

As such the Song takes us back to the early chapters of Genesis, in which God created male and female (Gen. 1:26, 27; 2:18-23) and joined them together in marriage, that they might "become one flesh" (2:24) through uniting not only their bodies in the sexual act but in terms of their entire lives. Sex, sexuality, and the human body had not yet at creation taken on their negative and perverted connotations. That would begin with the Fall of Genesis 3. Subsequently humanity would misuse and abuse God's good gift. But the good news is that all was not lost. Marriage, the book of Hebrews tells us, may still "be held in honor" and the marriage bed may still be "undefiled" (13:4). And Paul counsels husbands and wives to "satisfy the other's" sexual "needs" (1 Cor. 7:3, 5, TEV).

Sexuality and the marital relationship since Eden may have their difficult times (see, e.g., S. of Sol. 2:15; 5:6), but they are still important and enjoyable parts of God's creation. The Song of Solomon is God's reminder of that fact. It is an antidote to less than adequate views of the joys of human sexuality.

The Song's Literary Characteristics

The first thing to note in regard to the Song's literary characteristics is that it consistently employs figurative language more than any other Old Testament book. The language is not only metaphorical but often fluid in its usage of figures. Thus, for example, "vineyard" may refer to a place to grow grapes, to the girl as a whole in all her femininity, or it may be more explicitly sexual. Overall the Song's handling of language tends at times to leave readers with an impression of what is happening or being described rather than with an exact visualization. It is unfortunate that translation deletes much of the force of the original Hebrew, particularly the subtle word plays.

Repetition is another literary feature that even a casual reader of the Song will soon pick up. The book repeatedly raises various themes. For example, we find several refrains addressed to the daughters of Jerusalem (2:7; 3:5; 5:8; 8:4). Also, numerous phrases and sentences recur in identical or nearly identical form throughout the Song as it seeks to create atmosphere. Thus we find such repetitions as eyes like doves (1:15; 4:1), grazing among the lilies (2:16; 4:5; 6:3), mountains of spices (4:6; 8:14), and so on.

A third thing to note about the Song's literary character is that the type of love poems it contains were not unique to Israel. We have extant Canaanite, Mesopotamian, and Egyptian love poems. The closest in type to the Song of Solomon is the Egyptian. Those from Canaan and Mesopotamia are nearly always associated with fertility-cult rituals, while those from Egypt consist of non-cultic love poetry. Comparison between the Egyptian poems with the Song often provides revealing insights.

The Song also employs fantasy as a literary device. It appears that in such graphic, sexually explicit scenes as those found in Song of Solomon 2:3-6 and 3:1-4 the author has the female fantasizing future delights as she anticipates marriage. Lovers down through the ages have shared her experience by the hour.

Another literary technique that we should note is that of graphic imagery.

For example, the lovers never cease to compare each other's bodily parts to doves, vineyards, and so on. While such images were undoubtedly a source of the Song's power in that culture, modern Westerners often find those very images distasteful. Not many wives, for instance, would be flattered if their husband called them a horse or compared them to "a mare of Pharaoh's chariots" (1:9, RSV) or let them know that their neck reminded them of "the tower of David, . . . on which are hung a thousand shields" (4:4).

Modern readers need to realize that the canons of beauty change over time. One only has to think of the roly poly nudes of the renaissance period of Western art to realize that Hollywood has defined feminine beauty in a different way. Readers of the Song should recognize the verbal graphics as being for a time long gone. We might say the same things about our beloved in the twenty-first century but we would substitute our own images.

A final literary device used by the Song is stylized forms of love poetry. Among them are *descriptive songs,* in which each lover describes the other; *songs of yearning,* in which they express their ardent desire; *search narratives,* in which the woman recounts her frantic quest for her lover; *songs of admiration,* which focus on the beloved's dress or physical attributes; *self-descriptions,* used by the woman to make statements about herself; and *calls to oath,* imposed upon the daughters of Jerusalem. The Song has still other stylized forms, but the preceding examples help us begin to see the breadth of this literary technique (see, e.g., La Sor, pp. 603-605).

The Song's Major Themes

The Song of Solomon centers around the love relationship and the desire that the man and woman share. Sexuality is never far from the surface, but it is not an external or merely physical sexuality. The book's multifaceted approach falls short of a theology of sexuality, but it does highlight the fact that biblical sexuality is integrated into the complexity of a well rounded relationship. I am largely indebted to Richard Davidson for the following list of themes related to sexuality in this Best of Songs (see R. M. Davidson, pp. 6-17).

1. *Sexuality is good.* The Song's canonical status demonstrates that the sensual part of life is neither evil nor subhuman. To the contrary, it is one of God's special gifts. F. B. Knutson asserts that "this book's place in the Scriptures frustrates any attempt to denigrate the sensual aspect of human

life. The poems of Canticles express in artistic, colorful, joyful terms what is expressed in the creation story—'male and female he created them . . . and it was very good'" (in Bromiley, vol. I, p. 608).

2. *Sexuality is for couples*. Mutual commitment and exclusiveness form the main flow of the text throughout the Song. Song of Solomon 3:6-5:1, the book's emphatic center, makes it clear that it celebrates married love. We are not dealing with an extramarital affair or premarital experimentation but with a committed pair who have no desire for any other. David Hubbard writes that "no effort is spared, no literary device is left idle in making clear that the partners are pledged fully to each other and only to each other. *Metaphors* of exclusiveness (4:12-5:1; 4:4; 7:5), *vows* of exclusiveness (2:16; 6:3; 7:10), a *game* of exclusiveness (5:2-6:3), a test of exclusiveness (8:8, 9), *yearning* for exclusiveness (8:6, 7), *boasts* of exclusiveness (she: 8:10; he: 8:11, 12)—these combine to form a theme so dominant that it can rightly be called the main melody of the poems" (Hubbard, p. 262).

3. *Sexuality is egalitarian*. The Song does not portray a dominant, active male and a submissive, passive female. To the contrary, their relationship is more like a partnership of equals. Neither the male nor the female is reticent about taking the initiative. And neither is ashamed to express their longing for love. Whereas one might expect more from the male, in the Song of Songs the female supplies nearly twice as many verses as her lover. In fact, the Song provides a stronger female voice in dialogue than does any other biblical book.

In the Song we encounter a couple that mirrors the equality of the sexes as found in Genesis 2. Reflecting upon Genesis 2:21-25, the eighteenth-century commentator Matthew Henry notes that "the woman was *made of a rib out of the side of Adam;* not made out of his head to rule over him, nor out of his feet to be trampled upon by him, but out of his side to be equal with him, under his arm to be protected, and near his heart to be beloved" (Henry, p. 10). It is that sort of Edenic egalitarianism that appears in the Song of Songs.

4. *Sexuality is related to wholeness*. From the beginning of the Song to its end the lovers need each other. As in the Genesis picture they complement each other in a unified wholeness. The book presents them as individuals, but individuals in the "one flesh" unity of Genesis 2:24. They find

completeness in each other.

5. *Sexuality in a multidimensional relationship.* Another way of saying it is that the Song portrays sexuality as being more than sex. "Marriage is to a person, not to a body" (Hubbard, p. 262). Going beyond the biological, the Song pictures two people who love to hear each other's voices and who reflect an emotional attachment to each other. They appear to be friends as well as lovers.

6. *Sexuality is pleasurable.* Richard Davidson points out that "one aspect" of sexuality "is not mentioned" in the Song. It contains "no reference to the procreative function of sexuality" as we find in Genesis 1:28 with all of its talk of multiplying, being fruitful, and filling the earth. "Lovemaking for the sake of love, not procreation, is the message of the Song" (R. M. Davidson, pp. 15, 16).

Richard Hess adds that "physical love" provides "the focus of the Song. . . . It is this unbridled desire, with its exclusive commitment, that forms the basis for the confession of 8:6-7: 'Love is as strong as death' (NIV)" (Hess, p. 33). As such this Best of Songs is a wholesale rejection of the ascetic ideal. "The ideal" was not "a man who could have sexual intercourse with his wife without passion and only for the sake of procreation. Passion is what the Song celebrates" (Garrett, *Song*, p. 102).

7. *Sexuality is beautiful.* In truly exquisite language the Song of Solomon describes sexuality not as something ugly or dirty, but as utterly beautiful. Couched in terms of an Eden-like garden, the Song speaks to all five senses as its language pictures love as being sweet to the taste (2:3; 4:16), fragrant to the nose (2:13; 3:6; 4:16; 5:13), delightful to the touch (1:2; 2:3-6; 4:10, 11), exciting to the sight (4:9; 6:13), and thrilling to the ears (5:2). Symbolic descriptions of the beauty of human love and sexuality permeate the book.

8. *Post-fall sexuality is not without tension.* After all, there are the "little foxes that spoil the vineyards" (2:15, RSV), the times of absence that bring anxiety (3:1-4; 6:1), and uncoordinated peaks of desire that bring their own frustrations (5:2-6). But in the Song the couple transcends such difficulties and annoyances through an in-depth, multifaceted love that does not let life's problems and tensions devastate it.

9. *Sexuality reflects on God's love.* In the context of Scripture human love and sexuality are no accident. They originated with the Edenic cre-

ation of Genesis 1 and 2, in which human love finds its roots in the divine. Thus the human love in the Best of Songs points beyond itself to the greater Lover, the giver of "every perfect gift" (James 1:17). "Sex," writes Hess, "enables an experience of love whose intensity has no parallel in this cosmos and serves as a signpost to point to the greater love that lies beyond it" (Hess, p. 35).

And Richard Davidson adds that "the Song of Songs in its plain and *literal* sense is *not* just a 'secular' love song, but is fraught with deep spiritual, theological significance. From the OT Hebrew perspective God is not absent from the Song, nor are his love and concern for his creatures lacking in it. Rather, they are clearly shown in the enjoyment and pleasure (given by God to man in the creation) which the lovers find in each other and in their surroundings." Thus human sexuality "speaks eloquently" of God's "love for his creation as it is enjoyed in harmony with the divine intention" (R. M. Davidson, pp. 17, 18).

Structure of the Song

The structure of the Song has been an ongoing topic of debate among experts. The basic dividing line is whether "the eight chapters as they stand are a unit, composed of a relatively small number of poems, or the chapters are an anthology of disparate poems (even of a verse in length) that have been assembled with only the slightest unity" (Murphy, *Wisdom Literature,* p. 99). Even after that issue has been settled, there is still little consensus regarding the precise divisions of the text.

The present commentary, following a fairly well-beaten path (see, e.g., Hess, pp. 35, 36; Gledhill, pp. [9-11]; Bergant, pp. [v, vi]; Hubbard, pp. 265, 266; and each with one variation—Carr, pp. 68, 69; Delitzsch, p. 10; Balchin, p. 580; and Woudstra, p. 596), regards the book as consisting of six major poems. Hubbard suggests that the six poems are "put together in a sequence that builds from anticipation (Poems I-II) to consummation (Poem III) to aftermath (Poems IV-VI)." He goes on to suggest that "the nuptial festivities themselves seem to center in Poems III and V, with Poems I-II serving as introduction, Poem VI as conclusion, and Poem IV as interlude. No true plot is discernable, only a sense of movement or direction" (Hubbard, pp. 257, 258).

Central to the movement of the poems is the character cast, which we may divide into four subsets:

1. *The lovers.* The main focus centers on a young man and a young woman who are deeply in love. Some have sought to add a second male in a dramatic interpretation that sees a troublesome love triangle running throughout the book (see Longman, pp. 41-43). But a careful reading of the Song finds an account of the relationship of two lovers, with nothing in the text supporting the love-triangle approach.

Roland Murphy suggests that "the glue that holds" the poems "together is dialogue between the man and the woman" (Murphy, "Song," p. 242). Unfortunately, it is at times very difficult to tell which voice is which person. The good news is that in about 90 percent of the cases the Hebrew text has gender indicators that let us know who is speaking. Thus the problem is greater in English than Hebrew. The commentary that follows will utilize the gender indicators as it expounds upon the dialogue between the lovers.

2. *The "daughters of Jerusalem."* When mentioned by name the young women nearly always function as a backdrop for the speeches of the female (1:5; 2:7; 3:5, 11; 5:8, 16; 8:4). In the singular exception to the backdrop function they help her prepare for the wedding (3:10). When the daughters are present without being named they serve as a chorus whose words aid the poems to transition from one scene to another (5:1b, 9; 6:1, 13; 8:5a).

3. *The woman's brothers* (1:5, 6; 8:8-9) *and mother* (3:4; 6:9). The brothers appear to have a protective function (a role usually performed by a girl's father), while one of the references to the mother has parenting implications (6:9) and the other sexual (3:4).

4. *The watchmen* (3:3; 5:7). Mentioned twice, once in a neutral light and once as oppressors, the night watchmen occupy a place in the woman's dreams or fantasies.

As noted above, the main flow of the poems focuses on the words, thoughts, and deeds of the young lovers. The other characters appear from time to time on the sidelines of the action.

Outline of the Song

I. Title and attribution (1:1)

II. Poem I: Mutual yearning (1:2-2:7)
   A. Female: First invitation and shy uncertainty (1:2-7)
   B. Male: Response with invitation and praise (1:8-11)
   C. Female: The fragrance of love (1:12-14)
   D. Male and female: Lovers' banter (1:15-2:2)
   E. Female: Fantasy encounter (2:3-6)
   F. Female: Call for patience (2:7)

III. Poem II: Moving toward relationship (2:8-3:5)
   A. Female: The male's approach (2:8-10a)
   B. Male: First invitation (2:10b-14)
   C. Couple: Protecting their love (2:15)
   D. Female: Response with invitation (2:16, 17)
   E. Female: Fantasy search (3:1-5)

IV. Poem III: Love and marriage (3:6-5:1)
   A. Female: Groom's arrival (3:6-11)
   B. Male: Description of the bride (4:1-7)
   C. Male: Invitation to the bride (4:8)
   D. Male: Admiration of the bride (4:9-15)
   E. Female: Invitation to full intimacy (4:16)
   F. Male: Tasting the fruits of love (5:1a)
   G. Chorus: Enjoy your intimacy (5:1b)

V. Poem IV: Frustration and delight (5:2-6:3)
   A. Female: A troubling dream (5:2-7)
   B. Female: Call for help (5:8)
   C. Chorus: Teasing question (5:9)
   D. Female: Description of the male (5:10-16)
   E. Chorus: Teasing question (6:1)
   F. Female: More intimate enjoyment (6:2, 3)

VI. Poem V: Marital dynamics (6:4-8:4)
   A. Male: Description of the female (6:4-10)
   B. Female (?): Fantasy separation (6:11, 12)
   C. Chorus: Call to return (6:13)
   D. Male: Description of the female (7:1-5)
   E. Male: Yearning for intimacy (7:6-9)

The Song's Relevance for the Twenty-first Century

What could be more relevant than a God-given book on human sexuality? Here is a topic every person, for one reason or another, has or has had an interest in. Human sexuality is "a very fundamental part of our common humanity. The Song of Songs is an unabashed celebration of these deeply rooted urges" (Gledhill, p. 13). Read within the context of Scripture, the Song affirms love and sex within the bounds of marriage. But it is more than affirmation—it is a joyful celebration of physical love and committed relationships between men and women.

In its liberating function the Song pronounces that sex is good and God-given, thus freeing people from their hang-ups related to the idea that anything so pleasurable must be evil. The book "avoids both extremes of the cheapening of sex into promiscuity and of the locking away of this gift, never to be mentioned or appreciated for what it is" (Hess, p. 11). The Song teaches us that both men and women can be open and honest about their sexual desires and fears. And please note the emphasis in the Song on female assertiveness. For too long has Western culture treated sexuality as a male prerogative. The Song is a forceful and explicit correction of that fallacy.

Hope is another aspect of this very special book's relevance. We humans live in a fallen world with few islands of peace and security. The Best of Songs offers insight on how healthy, committed couples can capture a bit of Eden in their earthly lives. Such couples may, like Adam and Eve, become "one flesh" and be "naked" and "not ashamed" (Gen. 2:24, 25, RSV). Echoes of Eden roll through the Song. And in our God-given sexuality we find a foretaste of healings yet to come.

But we are not fully in the kingdom yet. And our present relationships have post-Fall problems. Thus the Song, like the rest of the Bible, pictures human sexuality even at its best as still being less than perfect. The lovers in the Song experience the pain of separation, the fear of loss, and misunderstandings that get magnified out of proportion. Their relationship may be a bit of Eden but it is also a bit of Earth. That revelation and realization is important to both those of us who are in the midst of a relationship and to those who in rosy-eyed expectation look forward to their own marriage. The Song cautions us not to expect too much.

A final point of relevance to note is that the Song helps us integrate our sexual selves with our relationship with God. "If the presence of the Song in the biblical canon suggests anything," Duane Garrett points out, "it is this: loving God with one's heart and soul and loving a member of the opposite sex with one's heart and flesh are not opposed to one another" (Garrett, *Song*, p. 101). The reading of the Song should lead us to praise our Creator, who not only fashioned us intricately as male and female but also planted within us the desire for sexual fulfillment and the sensory receptors that allow us to fully enjoy His gift.

Looking back at the Best of Songs, one author has written that "this is a song which Adam could have sung in Paradise" (Woudstra, p. 595). And so it is. But it is also a song we need to learn to sing today.

List of Works Cited

Balchin, John A. "The Song of Solomon." In *The New Bible Commentary*, rev. ed. D. Guthrie and J. A. Motyer, eds. Grand Rapids: Eerdmans, 1970, pp. 579-587.

Bergant, Dianne. *The Song of Songs*. Berit Olam, Studies in Hebrew Narrative and Poetry. Collegeville, Minn. Liturgical Press, 2001.

Bromiley, Geoffrey W., ed. *The International Standard Bible Encyclopedia*, rev. ed. 4 vols. Grand Rapids: Eerdmans, 1979-1988.

Carr, G. Lloyd. *The Song of Solomon*. Tyndale Old Testament Commentaries. Downers Grove, Ill.: Inter-Varsity, 1984.

Davidson, Richard M. "Theology of Sexuality in the Song of Songs: Return to Eden," *Andrews University Seminary Studies* 27:1 (Spring 1989):1-19.

Davidson, Robert. *Ecclesiastes and the Song of Solomon*. The Daily Study Bible. Louisville: Westminster John Knox, 1986.

Davis, Ellen F. *Proverbs, Ecclesiastes, and the Song of Songs*. Westminster Bible Companion. Louisville: Westminster John Knox, 2000.

Delitzsch, Franz. *Commentary on the Song of Songs and Ecclesiastes*. M. G. Easton, trans. Grand

Rapids: Eerdmans, n.d.

Ehlke, Roland Cap. *Ecclesiastes, Song of Songs*. St. Louis: Concordia, 1994.

Eusebius, *The History of the Church From Christ to Constantine*, G. A. Williamson, trans. New York: Penguin Classics, 1965.

Freedman, David Noel, ed. *The Anchor Bible Dictionary*, 6 vols. New York: Doubleday, 1992.

Garrett, Duane A. *Proverbs, Ecclesiastes, Song of Songs*. The New American Commentary. Nashville: Broadman, 1993.

Garrett, Duane and Paul R. House. *Song of Songs, Lamentations*. Word Biblical Commentary. Nashville: Thomas Nelson, 2004.

Gledhill, Tom. *The Message of the Song of Songs: The Lyrics of Love*. The Bible Speaks Today. Downers Grove, Ill.: Inter-Varsity, 1994.

Harris, R. Laird, Gleason L. Archer, Jr., and Bruce K. Waltke, eds. *Theological Wordbook of the Old Testament*, 2 vols. Chicago: Moody, 1980.

Henry, Matthew. *Matthew Henry's Commentary on the Whole Bible*. Complete and unabridged in one volume. Peabody, Mass.: Hendrickson, 1991.

Hess, Richard S. *Song of Songs*. Baker Commentary on the Old Testament Wisdom and Psalms. Grand Rapids: Baker Academic, 2005.

Hubbard, David A. *Ecclesiastes, Song of Solomon*. The Communicator's Commentary. Dallas: Word, 1991.

Jensen, Robert W. *Song of Songs*. Interpretation: A Bible Commentary for Teaching and Preaching. Louisville: John Knox, 2005.

Keel, Othmar. *The Song of Songs*. Frederick J. Gaiser, trans. A Continental Commentary. Minneapolis: Fortress, 1994.

Kinlaw, Dennis F. "Song of Songs." In *The Expositor's Bible Commentary*, Frank E. Gaebelein, ed. Grand Rapids: Zondervan, 1991, vol. 5, pp. 1199-1244.

Knight, George A. F. and Friedemann W. Golka, *Revelation of God: A Commentary on the Books of the Song of Songs and Jonah*. International Theological Commentary. Grand Rapids: Eerdmans, 1988.

La Sor, William Sanford, David Allen Hubbard, and Frederic Wm. Bush, *Old Testament Survey: The Message, Form, and Background of the Old Testament*. Grand Rapids: Eerdmans, 1982.

Lewis, C. S. *A Grief Observed*. New York: Bantam, 1976.

Longman, Tremper, III. *Song of Songs*. The New International Commentary on the Old Testament. Grand Rapids: Eerdmans, 2001.

Mishnah: A New Translation. Jacob Neusner, trans. New Haven, Conn.: Yale, 1988.

Murphy, Roland E. "Song of Solomon." In *The Books of the Bible*, vol. I, Bernhard W. Anderson, ed. New York: Charles Scribner's Sons, 1989, pp. 241-246.

———. *The Song of Songs*. Hermeneia—A Critical and Historical Commentary on the Bible. Minneapolis: Fortress, 1990.

———. *The Tree of Life: An Exploration of Biblical Wisdom Literature*. New York: Doubleday, 1990.

————. *Wisdom Literature: Job, Proverbs, Ruth, Canticles, Ecclesiastes, and Esther.* The Forms of the Old Testament Literature, vol. 13. Grand Rapids: Eerdmans, 1981.

Norris, Richard A., Jr., ed. and trans. *The Song of Songs: Interpreted by Early Christian and Medieval Commentators.* The Church's Bible. Grand Rapids: Eerdmans, 2003.

Pope, Marvin H. *Song of Songs.* The Anchor Bible. New York: Doubleday, 1977.

Snaith, John G. *The Song of Songs.* New Century Bible Commentary. Grand Rapids: Eerdmans, 1993.

Walsh, Carey Ellen. *Exquisite Desire: Religion, the Erotic, and the Song of Songs.* Minneapolis: Fortress, 2000.

Walton, John H., Victor H. Matthews, and Mark W. Chavalas. *The IVP Bible Background Commentary: Old Testament.* Downers Grove, Ill.: InterVarsity, 2000.

Weems, Renita J. "The Song of Songs: Introduction, Commentary, and Reflections." In *The New Interpreter's Bible,* Leander E. Keck, ed. Nashville, Tenn.: Abingdon, 1997, vol. 5, pp. 361-434.

Wittschiebe, Charles. *God Invented Sex.* Nashville: Southern Publishing Assn., 1974.

Woudstra, Sierd. "Song of Solomon." In *The Wycliffe Bible Commentary,* C. F. Pfeiffer and E. F. Harrison, eds. Chicago: Moody, 1962, pp. 595-604.

Wright, J. Robert, ed. *Proverbs, Ecclesiastes, Song of Solomon.* Ancient Christian Commentary on Scripture. Downers Grove, Ill.: InterVarsity, 2005.

Young, Edward J. *An Introduction to the Old Testament,* rev. ed. Grand Rapids: Eerdmans, 1960.

Part I

Preliminary Matters

Song of Solomon 1:1

1. What's So Good About This Song?

Song of Solomon 1:1
   ¹The Song of Songs, which is Solomon's.

Singing was important in ancient Israel. The prohibition against images prevented the Jewish people from developing an impressive tradition of visual art, such as we find in Greece, but the realm of music and song had no such limitations. Job 38:7 reflects upon singing at creation: "when the morning stars sang together, and all the sons of God shouted for joy" (RSV). Here we encounter singing in terms of celebration.

Following that lead, the great events of Jewish history find expression in song. Exodus 15, for example, sets forth the victorious songs of Moses (verses 1-18) and Miriam (verses 19-21), celebrating God's deliverance of Israel from Egypt. In a similar vein, Judges 5 praises God for His victories and 1 Samuel 2:1-10 presents Hannah's song of gratitude for the gift of Samuel. Other songs were for the instruction of God's people, such as that of Deuteronomy 31:30-32:47, that they might not forget His words. And we should never forget that the longest book in the Bible, Psalms, is a collection of songs for use on various occasions.

The New Testament carries on the vocal tradition of the Old. The gospel era begins with the song of Mary magnifying the Lord's goodness (Luke 1:46-56), Zechariah singing of God's salvation (1:67-80), the heavenly angels proclaiming

"Glory to God in the highest,
And on earth peace among men
with whom He is pleased" (2:14),

and Simeon voicing his thankfulness to God for letting him behold the Savior (2:29-35).

The last book of the New Testament also features singing. Revelation 5 pictures the heavenly beings bursting forth in a "new song" of victory, saying, "Worthy art thou" (verses 9, 10, RSV) and the fourteenth chapter has the 144,000 caught up in a song of deliverance (verse 3). In Revelation 15:3 the new song of chapter 5 and the deliverance song of chapter 14 are apparently conflated into the song of Moses and the Lamb.

Singing has been central to God's people all through biblical history. But it didn't stop there. Church history is full of the impact of songs and hymns as God's people have had occasions to praise His name and learn from His Word.

Those thoughts bring us back to the first verse of the Song of Solomon: "The Song of Songs, which is Solomon's." As we noted in the introduction, the Hebrew name for the Song comes from its first words: "Song of Songs." The Hebrew language, as we saw earlier, has no superlative. That is, it has no way of saying "the best" or "the most" as we do in English. The way Hebrew expresses such ideas is to repeat the word. We saw that in the book of Ecclesiastes, which uses the phrase "vanity of vanities" (1:2; 12:8) to indicate that which is the most vain, absurd, or meaningless. Thus when the ancient Hebrews wanted to describe the most important king they spoke of the "king of kings" or to name the most important part of God's sanctuary they called it the "holy of holies," that is, the most holy place of all holy places.

We find the same phenomenon in the first verse of the Song, in which the book describes itself as the "Song of Songs." An ancient Hebrew reader would see in that title a meaning similar to "the Best of Songs" or "the Best of all Songs" or "the Best Song of all."

That interpretation of "bestness" appears in the saying of Rabbi Akiba, who declared about A.D. 100 that "the entire age is not so worthy as the day on which the Song of Songs was given to Israel. For all the scriptures are holy, but the Song of Songs is holiest of all" (*Mishnah*, Yadayim 3:5).

The Targum (an Aramaic paraphrase of the Hebrew Scriptures) offered the same sentiment centuries later when it introduced the Song with the following words: "Ten songs were uttered in this world. This song was the best of them all" (quoted in Pope, p. 296). Those 10 songs, listed in the Targum, represented biblical songs about the great events and deliverances in Israel's history. Yet the Targum declared the Song of Solomon as the best.

Why, we are forced to ask, is that so? How can it be the best? Couldn't they come up with a better choice, perhaps one of the great hymns of praise such as Psalm 19 or 100? Have you read the Song of Songs lately? Have you evaluated its explicitly sexual conduct? Is this something you

---

How Can This Song Be the "Best"?

"Those who read it for a first time, or perhaps for a first time with full attention, may be surprised by what they find, for its overt content is very different . . . from that of any other book in the Bible. They will find neither ethical-theological reflection as in Job, nor exemplification of that fear of the Lord which is wisdom, as in the Psalms, nor the dicta of sages as in Proverbs or Ecclesiastes—and assuredly not history of salvation or torah or prophecy as in the rest of the Old Testament. Instead, they will find explicit . . . poetry of physical love. . . . The opening lines set the tone for the whole: without identification or preamble a woman cries, 'Let him kiss me with the kisses of his mouth.' . . . She is, as twelfth-century commentator William of St. Thierry wrote, with a mixture of fascination and alarm, 'wholly without modesty'" (Jenson, p. 1).

---

would want to read to your children for evening worship?

The answer to the bestness of the Song of Solomon, Richard Hess asserts, "lies in a careful study of the song and an understanding of the physical love praised here as sharing in the greater love of God, which he created for all those in his image to enjoy." If, Hess continues, the physical love praised in the Song is "separate from the greater spiritual love, then either the title is misleading or its author valued the carnal pleasures of sex above anything else." Hess is undoubtedly correct when he claims that "all the words and desires of the lovers point toward an understanding of love in which this song shares. The apostle may have reflected on such a knowledge when he concluded, 'The greatest of these is love' (1 Cor. 13:13, NIV)" (Hess, pp. 37, 38). Such an understanding not only mirrors the general tenor of Scripture, but it helps us recognize how the Song of Solomon could be the Best of Songs.

In the above discussion we saw how songs were at the center of the Bible from the beginning of recorded history. The same can be said for marriage. David Hubbard notes that "the Bible is about marriage" (Hubbard, p. 267). The Bible's first chapters introduce us to Adam and Eve whom God commanded to become "one flesh" and who were both naked, but were "not ashamed" (Gen. 2:24, 25). And the Bible story in its last few chapters climaxes with "the marriage of the Lamb" (Rev. 19:7). In between Genesis and Revelation Scripture continues to feature marriage, portraying Israel as God's spouse (see Hosea) and Jesus as the bridegroom (Matt. 19:14, 15), and comparing the relationship of a man to his wife to Christ's love for the church (Eph. 5:21-33).

It is in the middle of that marriage filled book that we find the collection of poems or wedding songs that we call the Song of Solomon. The Song, Hubbard reminds us, contains no worship liturgy, no commandments, no prophetic visions. Rather, "they are love songs pure and simple, bursting with passion, bright with desire, explosive with longing for physical love." They differ from all the rest of the Old Testament. "From Genesis 4 and 10 to the end of Malachi, sex is for begetting. . . . But the Song of Songs is different. Here sex is for joy, for union, for relationship, for celebration. Its lyrics contain no aspirations to pregnancy, no anticipations of parenthood" (Hubbard, p. 268). Rather, as we noted in our introduction, the joyful sex portrayed in the Song is a bit of Eden restored. Moving back beyond the perversions that have fractured sexuality beginning with the Fall of Genesis 3, the Song enables us to see with inspired insight what God made married life to be. As a result, "no part of Scripture sheds more light on what redeemed marital love can mean than the Song of Songs" (*ibid.,* p. 269). Thus the bestness of the Song resides in the fact that it presents the best subject.

Thus far in our discussion we have spent a great deal of time on the "Song of Songs" part of verse 1. We now need to examine the "which is

Solomon's" clause. Most readers have interpreted that phrase to mean that Solomon is the author. And taken in the context of 1 Kings 4 that seems to be a likely conclusion: "And God gave Solomon wisdom and understanding beyond measure, and largeness of mind like the sand on the seashore. . . . He also uttered three thousand proverbs; and his songs were a thousand and five" (verses 29, 32, RSV).

Having said that, we should note that "The Song of Songs, which is Solomon's" may not be referring to authorship. "Which is Solomon's" may have at least five meanings:

1. authorship,
2. ownership (being a part of the royal holdings),
3. dedication (written in Solomon's honor),
4. character (composed in the style of the king), or
5. subject (dealing with Solomon's experiences).

Because of such ambiguity it should be obvious that it cannot be proven from the text of the Song of Songs that Solomon was the author. Neither can it be disproved. But the good news is that the message of the Song does not depend upon authorship.

The Song mentions Solomon's name seven times (1:1, 5; 3:7, 9, 11; 8:11, 12) and five times it refers to the male figure as "king" (1:4, 12; 3:9, 11; 7:5). But we should also point out that the book also calls the same male figure a shepherd (1:7). Now while it is true that David had been both a shepherd and a king, the same cannot be said of Solomon. And Solomon, with his 700 wives and 300 concubines (1 Kings 11:3) is hardly a good example of the ideal committed husband that we find in the Song, whose bride can declare "my beloved is mine and I am his" (2:16 cf. 6:3; 7:10).

Rather than picturing one of Solomon's romances, it is more likely that the Song utilized royal imagery to highlight the pomp and dignity that surrounds a young couple on their marriage day. That has been true across time. In our day, for example, a young couple might exist in blue jeans and torn shirts up to the event itself. But at that point the young man dons a tuxedo of princely style while the young woman puts on a flowing gown with a veil and crown. And everyone rises in honor as she enters in queenly style to be united to her prince charming. They are king and queen for a day. But on the next it is back to blue jeans and working as a shepherd or grocery clerk. Not all that much has changed since the days of Solomon. Weddings are still royal affairs that often need a royal budget to pay for them.

The important thing in the Song is not any historical characters or specific events in time but the love and honor represented in God's gift of committed coupleness. In spite of its humanness and its lack of specific mention of God, the Song reflects Him all the way through. "It is about *human* love at its best," Hubbard comments. "But behind it, above it, and through it, the Song, as part of the divinely ordered repertoire of Scripture, is a paean of praise to the Lord of creation who makes possible such exquisite love and to the Lord of redemption who demonstrated love's fullness on a cross" (Hubbard, p. 274).

Part II

Moving Toward Intimacy

Song of Solomon 1:2-3:5

2. Yearnings Expressed
(Poem I, Part A)

Song of Solomon 1:2-11

[2] "May he kiss me the kisses
  of his mouth!
For your love is better than wine.
[3] "Your oils have a pleasing fragrance,
Your name is like purified oil;
Therefore the maidens love you.
[4] "Draw me after you and let us run
  together!
The king has brought me into his
  chambers."
"We will rejoice in you and be glad;
We will extol your love more
  than wine.
Rightly do they love you."
[5] "I am black but lovely,
O daughters of Jerusalem,
Like the tents of Kedar,
Like the curtains of Solomon.
[6] "Do not stare at me because I am
  swarthy,
For the sun has burned me.
My mother's sons were angry
  with me;
They made me caretaker of the
  vineyards,
But I have not taken care of my

own vineyard.
[7] *"Tell me, O you whom my soul*
loves,
Where do you pasture your flock,
Where do you make it lie down
at noon?
For why should I be like one who
veils herself
Beside the flocks of your companions?"

[8] *"If you yourself do not know,*
Most beautiful among women,
Go forth on the trail of the flock
And pasture your young goats
By the tents of the shepherds.
[9] *"To me, my darling, you are like*
My mare among the chariots of
Pharaoh.
[10] *"Your cheeks are lovely with ornaments,*
Your neck with strings of beads."
[11] *"We will make for you ornaments*
of gold
With beads of silver."

There is nothing backward about this young woman! She puts her cards on the table from the first words of the Song: "May he kiss me the kisses of his mouth!" (verse 2). Whatever thoughts we may have harbored about female reticence in the Bible, that statement puts them to rest. But not only here. She takes the verbal lead throughout the entire Song, uttering about two words for every one for the male. However, we should note one thing. She may be right up front in expressing her desires, but she expects him to lead out on the actual kissing: "May he kiss me."

Romantic kissing, by the way, is not a big topic in the Old Testament. In fact, Scripture makes few references to the subject. In Proverbs 7:13 it is a harlot who seduces a young man through kissing, and Song of Solomon 8:1 deals with the kissing of one's brother. But some students of the topic tell us that "a kiss on the lips was used as a passionate expression throughout the Near East, though Egyptians in the early periods often touched noses instead" (Walton, p. 576). The probable reason that we don't hear more specifically about romantic kissing in the Bible is that its focus is on other issues. Thus we can be thankful for the Song, which puts flesh on Old Testament characters that helps us identify with them more fully. We all enjoy reading about Abraham and Sarah and Rachel and Jacob, but the Song puts us one step closer to the sexual mores of their day. The sage might speak of the way of a man with a maid back in ancient Israel (Prov. 30:19), but the Song enables us to learn what those ways might have been. And we see from Song of Solomon 1:2 that this very open book helps us observe the way of a maid with a man. Some things may have changed quite a bit in the past three millennia, but apparently not human sexuality. At any rate, most of us can still get worked up about kissing our beloved.

In verse 3 the female offers her appreciation of the scent of his "oils." We would call it perfume. Please note that such perfumes were not a sign of effeminacy. We males still wear cologne. But for us in the twenty-first century it is an enhancer of our good smells. Throughout most of history, such oils served not only as enhancers but also "maskers." Daily bathing and deodorants are relatively recent inventions. Even as late as the 1830s the average American never took a bath their entire life. In such a context the good smelling oils took on added dimensions of meaning.

Not only did her lover physically smell good, so did his name. A good name stood for a good reputation, as it still does. Because of his qualities, our woman asserts, "the maidens love you" (verse 3). That is another way of saying that he is a valuable catch. All of us are interested in how others view our new date. And many a prospect has gotten dropped when the friends reply, "I can't see what you see in him (her)." No problem here in Song of Solomon. Everyone seems to like her lover.

Now there is something that many of us have discovered about kissing. One good kiss calls for another. The poet writes:

> "May I print a kiss on your lips?" I said.
> And she nodded her full permission;
> So we went to press and I rather guess
> We printed a full edition" (Joseph Lilienthal in Gledhill,
> p. 101).

So it goes in the Song. The girl in her imagination envisions the conclusion to which passionate kissing leads: "Draw me after you and let us
run together!" (verse 4). Now, beyond walking, she is ready to "run." The
"king," she fantasizes, "has brought me to his chambers." Which of us
hasn't had such thoughts as a relationship begins to develop. God made us
male and female and our bodies and imaginations race through various
possible scenarios with our beloved. The good news, according to the
Song, is that such musings are normal.

The mention of the king in verse 4, by the way, does not necessarily
infer royalty. After all, as we have already observed, verse 7 calls the same
young man a shepherd. Rather, it is most likely a literary device. He is *her*
king and she is *his* queen. Young women still search for their "prince charming." In addition, we have evidence that some ancient Near Eastern marriage
ceremonies, as in the Eastern Orthodox church today, viewed the young
couple as king and queen for the duration of their wedding festivities.

We can find a lesson here for every marriage. How much happier our
marriages would be if we treated our spouses with the honor and respect
of royalty. Not a bad idea. And it works both ways. Such a marriage will
enrich both partners.

In verses 5 and 6 the focus radically shifts. The woman is still speaking, but it is no longer about her beloved. Rather, she moves to a modest
self-description. She knows she is "lovely," but she also is aware of the fact
that she does not have the fair, cared-for skin of the pampered city girls.
Her complexion, ravaged by the sun, resembles the "tents of Kedar,"
woven from the hair of black goats. She claims that her brothers put her
in the fields because they were angry with her. The Song does not tell us
why they were angry, but from Song of Solomon 8:8, 9 it may have been
because they worried about her developing beauty and budding sexuality.
In order to protect her from herself and from men they put her out in the
vineyards where she not only kept busy but took on a deep tan, apparently
a sign that she belonged to the working class. The fact that the brothers
undertook the task of disciplining their sister most likely indicates that her
father had passed away. At any rate, Song of Solomon 1:5, 6 indicates a
modesty that is attractive in its own right.

With verse 7 she takes the offensive again, asking her shepherd boyfriend
where he pastures his flock so that she could pay him a noontime visit. The

last thing she wants to do, she tells him, is to go from shepherd to shepherd asking directions. "Why," she asks him, "should I be like one who veils herself" (verse 7). Her veiled presence in the field might mark her in their eyes as a prostitute, like Tamar when she set out to trap Judah (Gen. 38:14).

The male speaks for the first time in verse 8. Just play the part of a shepherd and tend your goats and no one will ask any questions, he replies. That is good advice, but the part of the verse that needs emphasizing is where he calls her "most beautiful among women." Do you really think that she was the "most beautiful"? I doubt it. But she was in his eyes. And, I might add, happy is the relationship in which every spouse sees his or her partner as something special. Of course in verse 8 the lover has in mind her modesty of verses 5 and 6, but there is something much deeper here. All of our spouses have their "warts," but if we can reinforce their good points our efforts often become a self-fulfilling prophecy. If we treat people as if they are stupid and ugly, they will tend to act that way. But if we show them how much we cherish, value, and appreciate them it will transform their smile, attitude, and every other part of their life. Happy is the husband or wife who can see their spouse as *the most*.

Of course, verse 9 doesn't seem all that flattering to a modern Western mind. I would not suggest that you compare your wife to a horse unless you have some alternate place to sleep and eat for a few years. But here we are dealing with an extremely important point in biblical imagery. What one society may deem a compliment another might regard as an insult.

Marvin Pope helps us see the mare analogy in a different light. He notes that chariot horses were usually stallions. He then describes a defense strategy in which one army releases a mare in heat among the charging chariots, thus detracting the stallions. Such a strategy was used in the Egyptian attack on Qadesh (Pope, pp. 336-341). With that picture in mind, by calling his beloved "a mare among the chariots of Pharaoh" (S. of Sol. 1:9) the male is "saying that she drives all men crazy with her attractiveness" (Longman, p. 103). While Pope's suggestion may or may not be the root of the imagery in verse 9, we can be assured that the lover in our story meant a compliment when he called his beloved a "mare among the chariots of Pharaoh." He may have merely been inferring that Pharaoh had the means to purchase the very best, and that she was in the top rank of women in his eyes.

The lover concludes his first song of admiration in verse 10 and 11, in which he further refutes her modest self-assessment of verses 5 and 6. His compliments continue the motif of royalty she used in verse 4. She was not only the best of the best and the most alluring, but she, in his eyes, had all the ornaments of a queen.

Song of Solomon 1:2-11 leaves us in no doubt that we are dealing with a couple in love with each other. The rest of Poem I (1:12-2:7) en-riches the picture of their appreciation of one another.

3. Building Passion
(Poem I, Part B)

Song of Solomon 1:12-2:7

> [12] *"While the king was at his table,*
> *My perfume gave forth its fragrance.*
> [13] *"My beloved is to me a pouch of myrrh*
> *Which lies all night between my breasts.*
> [14] *"My beloved is to me a cluster of*
> *henna blossoms*
> *In the vineyards of Engedi."*

> [15] *"How beautiful you are, my darling,*
> *How beautiful you are!*
> *Your eyes are like doves."*

> [16] *"How handsome you are my beloved,*
> *And so pleasant!*
> *Indeed, our couch is luxuriant!*
> [17] *"The beams of our houses are cedars,*
> *Our rafters, cypresses.*
> **2** *I am the rose of Sharon,*
> *the lily of the valleys."*

> [2] *"Like a lily among the thorns,*
> *So is my darling among the maidens."*

> [3] *"Like an apple tree among the trees*
> *of the forest,*
> *So is my beloved among the*

> *young men.*
> *In his shade I took great delight*
> *and sat down,*
> *And his fruit was sweet to my*
> *taste.*
> *⁴"He has brought me to his banquet*
> *hall,*
> *And his banner over me is love.*
> *⁵"Sustain me with raisin cakes,*
> *Refresh me with apples,*
> *Because I am lovesick.*
> *⁶"Let his left hand be under my*
> *head*
> *And his right hand embrace me."*
>
> *⁷"I adjure you, O daughters of*
> *Jerusalem,*
> *By the gazelles or by the hinds*
> *of the field,*
> *That you do not arouse or*
> *awaken my love*
> *Until she pleases."*

The first part of Poem I closed with a song of admiration from the young man (1:9-11). In verses 12-14 the female replies with her own admiration song. His song dealt with her value and beauty, while her's will move beyond his person to scenes of intimacy. She begins by picturing "her" king at his reclining couch, which could be used for either eating or love making. "Table" is an unfortunate translation that transfers the symbolism from a Near Eastern context to that of a modern dining room without making room for the fact that eating in ancient Israel took place in a reclining position. At any rate, she notes that her perfume was doing its job as it sent out its enticing smells (verse 12).

She continues on in verses 13 and 14 to picture her and her lover in an intimate situation. The two verses represent a parallel construction that we can picture as follows:

a   pouch of myrrh
b   my beloved is to me

c	which lies all night between my breasts
a[1]	cluster of henna blossoms
b[1]	my beloved is to me
c[1]	in the vineyards of Engedi

The picture is impressionistic. The young woman visualizes her lover as precious herbs that have their own beautiful smell, echoing the mention of her own perfume in verse 12. But it is the positioning of these special herbs that introduces her thoughts of intimacy.

Somewhat taken aback by the vividness of the scene, some Jewish and Christian interpreters of an earlier era allegorized the two breasts as the Old and New Testaments, with Christ being the perfume between them. But as Richard Hess points out, "there is no indication in the Song that this is intended as anything more than the deepest yearning of the female lover for her partner. In her musings she opens to him the most precious parts of her body" (Hess, p. 70).

To put it more bluntly, she desires her lover to spend the night with her pressed between her breasts. The parallel positioning of her statement regarding "the vineyards of Engedi" in verse 14 also points to sexual intimacy. In Song 1:6 she refers to her own person as a vineyard. Engedi, located about halfway down the western shore of the Dead Sea, was one of the region's most fruitful places, one at which David had hid while fleeing from Saul (1 Sam. 23:29; 24:1). Putting the pieces of the passage together, she depicts Engedi as a rural and private retreat where her lover can enjoy her vineyard.

"The explicit nature of portions of the Song of Songs may be a bit shocking to some readers. . . . Most English translations disguise some of the most blatant erotic imagery with euphemism and metaphor, as is appropriate considering the poetic nature of the literature and the need to preserve a certain propriety for a general audience" (Walton, p. 577).

The "king" finds his voice again in verse 15, but by this time the Song portrays him as being so star struck that he repeats himself, saying the same thing about her beauty more than once. But after the repetition he does throw in a simile about her eyes being like doves, an allusion we will see again in Song of Solomon 4:1 and 5:12. Pope suggests that the comparison with doves might refer to the "glistening color" and "quick movements" of the dove, as well as perhaps being a symbol of a sweet disposition and love (Pope, p. 356). If so, then the male is describing her whose love, vivacity, and desire is expressed in her eyes.

Verse 16 finds the young woman responding in kind, not only returning the compliment but adding a statement about the luxuriousness of their couch or bed. From verse 17 it is impossible to tell if the majestic setting of their apparently imagined hideaway is a royal room of expensive cedar and pine or a secret place in the forest. But the image symbolizes the quality of their relationship.

The female closes off her little speech by noting that she is "the rose of Sharon" and "the lily of the valleys" (2:1). Read through Christian eyes this could sound like she is uplifting her beauty and value. But from both the context in verse 2 and from what we know about these flowers it appears that she has entered into a second round of self-depreciation (cf. 1:5, 6), claiming that she is merely a common flower. Or as David Hubbard puts it, "No rare-bloom is she, no delicate hothouse specimen, but a plain, everyday blossom, readily plucked, sniffed, and tossed aside by an idle shepherd" (Hubbard, p. 286).

If such words are a subtle attempt at flirtation, she succeeds magnificently. Not so! her lover declares in verse 2. Compared with other young women she is like a graceful flower among thorns.

The bantering love talk continues in verse 3, with the young woman responding in kind, claiming that he too is no ordinary person. To the contrary, one may compare him to a valuable apple tree and not one of the common trees of the forest. The apple tree, of course, is superior because of both its fruit and its sweet smell. The rest of the trees of the forest are ordinary, but her lover is special.

As is often the case in the Song, the female forges beyond endearments to visions of intimacy in which she will raise the symbol of the apple tree again (see verse 5). In the second half of verse 3 she is happy to be under his protective care ("in his shade I took great delight"). From there she moves to another fantasy encounter of the deepest intimacy. "Their physical union," Tremper Longman notes, "is represented by the fact that she tastes his fruit" (Longman, p. 112).

Then she becomes more specific in verse 4, in which she imagines him taking her to "his banquet hall" and declares that "his banner over me is love." The exact significance of that last phrase is unclear, since the banner is a military metaphor, but the banner or military standard may signify possession. At any rate, the overall idea of what she expects to take place in the banqueting house is clear enough, especially when read in the context of verses 5 and 6.

Verse 6, with its portrayal of the man's left hand under her head while his right hand "embraces or fondles her" (Bergant, p. 26) is especially graphic as she fantasizes their possibilities. Her lovesickness of verse 5 can mean either that she is sick with thoughts of love or worn out from lovemaking. At any rate, her call for raisin cakes and apples are at least for physical refreshment, but they perhaps have symbolic overtones of sexual stimulation.

The counsel of verse 7 to the daughters of Jerusalem not to arouse or awaken love "until she pleases" or "until it pleases" (RSV) has perplexed students of the Song. Some see in it a caution to her female friends not to become overly involved until the time is right. That is good advice, but it seems that Tom Gledhill may be closer to the actual intent when he suggests that this passage, repeated with variations in Song of Solomon 3:5 and 8:4, is the girl calling for herself to slow things down. "She wants their love to be consummated," he writes, "but she is in great tension, because she knows that the time is not yet ripe. In speaking to the daughters of Jerusalem, she is speaking to herself. She is basically telling herself to cool it, to wait for the appropriate time." And that appropriate time, he adds, is marriage (Gledhill, p. 129).

Thus the girl's caution to the daughters of Jerusalem is important, not only for herself and for them but for all of us, especially to the unmarried and those marrieds who may find themselves "available" again in the future because of some personal tragedy in their lives. The problem is not with our desires or our physical sensations. Those are God given. What is wrong is when those drives take over and spiral people out of control as they seek to find fulfillment in illegitimate ways.

We have come to the end of Poem I. It has added dimensions to our views of biblical sexuality. And it lends credence to the title of a book by one of my seminary teachers: *God Invented Sex*. And He did! But back when Charles Wittschiebe published that title some of us weren't quite willing to openly admit God's involvement. We certainly weren't ready to shout it from the housetops. But that seems to be the very definite message of both the opening chapters of Genesis and, more graphically, the Song of Solomon from beginning to end. Poem I has shown us the yearnings and fantasizings of the two young people, but it has also pointed to the need for caution as passions become inflamed. We are now ready for Poem II, in which our young woman pictures the coming of her lover to bring the fantasies of Poem I to fruition.

4. The Dynamics of Love
(Poem II)

Song of Solomon 2:8-3:5

[8] *"Listen! My beloved!*
Behold, he is coming,
Climbing on the mountains,
Leaping on the hills!
[9] *"My beloved is like a gazelle or a*
young stag.
Behold, he is standing behind our wall,
He is looking through the windows,
He is peering through the lattice.

[10] *"My beloved responded and said to me,*
'Arise, my darling, my beautiful one,
And come along.
[11] *'For behold, the winter is past,*
The rain is over and gone.
[12] *'The flowers have already appeared*
in the land;
The time has arrived for pruning
the vines,
And the voice of the turtledove
has been heard in our land.
[13] *'The fig tree has ripened its figs,*
And the vines in blossom have
given forth their fragrance.
Arise, my darling, my beautiful one,
And come along!' "

[14] "O my dove, in the clefts of the rock,
In the secret place of the steep
        pathway,
Let me see your form,
Let me hear your voice;
For your voice is sweet
And your form is lovely."

[15] "Catch the foxes for us,
The little foxes that are ruining
        the vineyards,
While our vineyards are in
        blossom."

[16] "My beloved is mine, and I am his;
He pastures his flock among the lilies.
[17] "Until the cool of the day when the
        shadows flee away,
Turn, my beloved, and be like a
        gazelle
Or a young stag on the mountains
        of Bether."

3 "On my bed night after night I
        sought him
Whom my soul loves;
I sought him but did not find him.
[2] 'I must arise now and go about
        the city;
In the streets and in the squares
I must seek him whom my soul
        loves.'
I sought him but did not find him.
[3] "The watchmen who make the
        rounds on the city found me,
And I said, 'Have you seen him
        whom my soul loves?'
[4] "Scarcely had I left them
When I found him whom my soul
        loves;
I held on to him and would not
        let him go

> Until I had brought him to my
>   mother's house,
> And into the room of her who
>   conceived me."
>
> [5]"I adjure you, O daughters of
>   Jerusalem,
> By the gazelles or by the hinds
>   of the field,
> That you will not arouse or
>   awaken my love
> Until she pleases."

One thing that we can say for certain about the Song is that its language is graphic. Some of the symbolism and vocabulary might be obscure, but the book depicts what is going on in vivid Technicolor phrases.

The young lover in our poem is not a bit bashful or backward in his response to his "darling's" (1:9) invitations (1:4, 5; 2:3-6). She pictures him in his response as a fleet-footed gazelle or a young stag "leaping upon the mountains, bounding over the hills" (2:8, 9, RSV) as he seeks out her presence.

Those words and the boundless energy they express say it all. How excited I was as a young man as I neared my girlfriend's home. Leaping and bounding is how I felt, not only in my body but in my heart. Some of us today may be beyond the leaping stage but we know the enthusiasm expressed in the song. And things haven't changed all that much for modern Shulammites (see 6:13, in which the female receives this title). They still encourage attention (1:2-4) and listen for a response (2:8). Boldness is a part of being in love, but it isn't the whole story.

Verse 9 reveals the other half. It finds him standing outside her home, "looking through the windows, . . . peering through the lattice." A shyness replaces the boldness. He has arrived at her home but doesn't seem to know what to do. All the confidence of his imagination has dissipated now that reality has taken over. While he knows that he should do something, he ends up just staring voicelessly.

She knows he is there, and he realizes that she is aware of his presence, but he is having a difficult time whipping up his courage. After some pause his beloved tells us that he finally gets his act together, inviting her to arise and follow him (verse 10).

The invitation itself he couches in the imagery of spring, the time of fruitfulness, singing, and love. His words are well thought out and could hardly be more appealing to the lovesick young woman (2:5), whose desires were more than strong (2:3-6) and needed tempering to keep them under control (verse 7). At the end of the springtime description, her lover repeats the invitation to "arise . . . and come along" that she has been waiting to hear (verse 13).

Changes in Love Talk

"Song of Songs is an ideal text for comparing the changing history and context of romantic talk. The poet uses the language and imagery of a rustic, semi-pastoral culture to evoke passion and desire. Comparisons to goats, gazelles, and apple trees sound strange to those of us who reside in parts of the country where neighborhoods are treeless, apartment complexes have no lawns, and we ride underground in the earth's belly to get to our windowless downtown offices. . . . While it may be true that much of the speech of this little book is hopelessly lost on our modern ears . . . , we must admit that our own language for intimacy is equally lost on those unfamiliar with our culture. How does a generation flatter and woo one another when they are raised on microwave ovens, computers, fax machines, voice mail . . . ? How do they talk about love? 'You've pushed the right button,' perhaps. . . . The maiden and her suitor of the Song of Songs would stagger down the slopes of En-gedi in amazement and laughter at the sound of twenty-first century erotic speech" (Weems, p. 395).

But at that very point her own confidence ebbs as her own shyness overcomes her previous boldness. He notes in his appeal that she has become like a timid dove hiding in the clefts of the rocks. "Let me see your form, let me hear your voice" (verse 14). And in an effort to encourage her he adds flattering words about the beauty and sweetness of her body and voice.

The terminology of those scenes may be archaic and no longer reflect the symbols of our experience, but the rapidly changing emotions from desire to boldness to shyness and perhaps to desperation still echo the experience of most lovers 3,000 years later. We want but we don't want. We imagine but we can't act. And we have made up our minds but are not ready. Excitement is great but reality and commitment can be scary. That is true not only in our love attachments to other people, but also in committing ourselves to God, the Lover who makes all love possible. No one ever said love would be risk free. But a life without love loses a great part of its luster.

Verse 15 with its reference to little foxes that ruin vineyards brings several word pictures to mind. One is that of destructive foxes. Duane Garrett cites a few ancient documents that demonstrate that "foxes were notorious for their stealing of grapes from vineyards" (Garrett, *Song*, p. 160). As to vineyards, in Song of Solomon 1:6 and 8:12 the leading lady links her beauty to the idea of a vineyard that needs protection and care.

Reflecting on those symbols, David Hubbard suggests that the foxes represent "the ravages of the aging process that can sap the beauty and vitality of persons (the *'vines'* or vineyards)." That reading lets us see Song of Solomon 2:15 in the light of the oft repeated thought about the time being right (2:7, 13; 3:5; 7:12; 8:4). From that perspective, the couple in the verse are saying, "Let us give full expression to our love before aging *('the foxes')* takes its toll on our beauty and vigor *('spoil the vines')*" (Hubbard, p. 293).

With Song of Solomon 2:16, 17 we find the young woman speaking again. Perhaps the most important words in this short song are "my beloved is mine, and I am his," a phrase repeated exactly in 6:3 and paraphrased in 7:10. Those words are crucial to the interpretation of the Song of Solomon. They are "the language of ownership: she belongs to him and he belongs to her" (Longman, p. 125). The Song is not talking about flitting from one relationship or from one man or woman to another. Neither is it about the kind of polygamous marriages experienced by the "real Solomon." Rather, the implications of verse 16 conform to God's ideal set forth in Genesis 2:24 and reflected upon by Jesus, when He claimed that the "two [rather than the three or the six] shall become one flesh" (Matt. 19:5, RSV).

The opening words of verse 16, as we noted above, are crucial for interpreting the Song. We are dealing here with two deeply committed people. The book pictures them as mutually pledging themselves to each other, with no room for others. It is the language of possession, of a permanent relationship.

The young female finishes her song in verses 16 and 17 with an additional allusion to intimacy: "He pastures his flock among the lilies." Since "his flock" are supplied words not in the Hebrew, she is noting that "he feeds among the lilies." The personal nature of the pasturing or eating emerges when we remember that in Song of Solomon 2:1 she referred to herself as a lily. Verse 17 closes with an invitation to her "king" to "be like a gazelle or a young stag on the mountains." Mountains here are in all probability referring to her bodily contours.

With Song of Solomon 3:1-5 we arrive at a very definite shift of scenery as the young woman reports a dream. In her troubling night vision she finds herself being repaid for the elusiveness that bothered her lover in 2:14. There he appealed to her to come openly into his presence, but now it is she who searches for him in the give and take of love's romantic intrigues.

She dreams of leaving her house to hunt for him throughout the city (3:2). In her wanderings she encounters the watchmen who guard the city against troublesome outsiders, but they are of no help. On the other hand, they cause her no trouble as they do in a later dream (5:7). Soon after leaving them she finds her lover and forcefully compels him into her mother's bedroom (3:4).

To put it mildly, her dream presents her as "ready for action." Her nocturnal fantasies having carried her to the edge, she is primed for full intimacy.

But the time is not right. Once again (cf. 2:7) in conversing with the daughters of Jerusalem (3:5) she is actually speaking to herself, telling herself to cool it, to await the appropriate time (Gledhill, p. 129).

That time, however, will come, and in the flow of the Song of Solomon it happens in Poem III (3:6-5:1), which moves from the arrival of the groom in 3:6-11 to his tasting of the fruits of intimacy in 5:1.

Poem II (2:8-3:5), meanwhile, has heightened the tension of desire that began from the first verses of Poem I (1:2-2:7). But Poem II has not only intensified the desire, it also highlighted the idea of mutual and permanent commitment (2:16) and by the repeated use of "whom my soul loves" (four repetitions in 3:1-4) emphasized that love is not a mere physical, skin-deep infatuation. The Hebrew word for soul *(nepesh)* means more than some spiritual attribute of a person but the entire person (see Harris, vol. II, pp. 587-591). Thus the woman is saying that her love for her young man "is not simply her romantic interest alongside other life interests. Instead, it characterizes the whole of her existence. . . . The woman's soul [total being] is wholly invested in her lover" (Walsh, p. 78). Assuming that his experience is similar to hers, the progression of the Song is ready to move on to the consummation of their relationship in Poem III.

Happy is the marriage that not only has intensity of desire but mutual commitment and the kind of in-depth love toward one another that reflects the love God commands toward Himself. He asks us to love Him with all our heart, soul, and might (Deut. 6:4; cf. Matt. 22:34-40). Desire without commitment and soul-deep love leads to disaster, while commitment and soul-deep love without desire is much less than God's ideal for His children. But when all three combine we find the basis for marriage as He originally designed it.

Part III

Marriage Day

Song of Solomon 3:6–5:1

5. The Coming of the Groom
(Poem III, Part A)

Song of Solomon 3:6–4:7

> [6]*"What is this coming up from*
>   *the wilderness*
> *Like columns of smoke,*
> *Perfumed with myrrh and*
>   *frankincense,*
> *With all scented powders of the*
>   *merchant?*
> [7]*"Behold, it is the traveling couch*
>   *of Solomon;*
> *Sixty mighty men around it,*
> *Of the mighty men of Israel.*
> [8]*"All of them are wielders of the*
>   *sword,*
> *Expert in war;*
> *Each man has his sword at his*
>   *side,*
> *Guarding against the terrors of*
>   *the night.*
> [9]*"King Solomon has made for himself a*
>   *sedan chair*
> *From the timber of Lebanon.*
> [10]*"He made its posts of silver,*
> *Its back of gold*
> *And its seat of purple fabric*
> *With its interior lovingly fitted out*
> *By the daughters of Jerusalem.*

[11] *"Go forth, O daughters of Zion,*
And gaze on King Solomon with
the crown
With which his mother has
crowned him
On the day of his wedding,
And on the day of his gladness of
heart."

4 *"How beautiful you are, my*
darling,
How beautiful you are!
Your eyes are like doves behind
your veil;
Your hair is like a flock of goats
That have descended from Mount
Gilead.
[2] *"Your teeth are like a flock of*
newly shorn ewes
Which have come up from their
washing,
All of which bear twins,
And not one of them has
lost her young.
[3] *"Your lips are like a scarlet*
thread,
And your mouth is lovely,
Your temples are like a slice of a
pomegranate
Behind your veil.
[4] *"Your neck is like the tower of*
David,
Built with rows of stones
On which are hung a thousand
shields,
All the round shields of the
mighty men.
[5] *"Your two breasts are like two*
fawns,
Twins of a gazelle
Which feed among the lilies.
[6] *"Until the cool of the day*

When the shadows flee away,
I will go my way to the mountain
of myrrh
And to the hill of frankincense.
[7]"You are altogether beautiful, my
darling,
And there is no blemish in you."

There is nothing more exciting than a wedding day. Everyone dresses in their finest and are on their best behavior. In fact, you hardly recognize some of them, given their usual garb and demeanor. But the day is a special day, and everybody puts forth extra effort in honor of the bride and groom.

Those two are the center of attraction. Everyone wants to catch a glimpse of them. The groom shows up first, perhaps for the first time in his life in a tuxedo. And maybe his last. But it is his special day, and for it he dresses up like a head of state.

But if the groom is impressive, wait until you see the bride. She may be somewhat ordinary on most days, but on her wedding day she stands second to none, not even the fabled Queen of Sheba. As the music swells into the wedding march all rise to their feet, turning slightly, perhaps even standing on their tiptoes to get a good look at her. Of course, soon she will be up front standing next to the princely form of her soon-to-be husband.

Such are the ceremonies and symbolisms of modern marriage.

It appears that things haven't changed that much in three millennia. Pomp, ceremony, imagination, and specialness have apparently always surrounded wedding events.

The one pictured in Song of Solomon 3 and 4 is no different. In Song of Solomon 3:6 one of the royal couple is making a grand entry. Some students of the topic think it is the bride, others the groom. The puzzle does not get settled textually until verse 11, in which the bride speaks to the daughters of Zion (i.e., daughters of Jerusalem) regarding the groom. We know it is the bride speaking because she is the only one in the song to address that collection of women.

Thus in Song of Solomon 3:6-11 we find the grand entrance of the groom. The one described as nothing but a shepherd in 1:7 the book now pictures as royalty arriving in style. The stylistic symbolism in one sense isn't all that different from our day. A young couple that usually drives a 15-year-old bottom-of-the-line Chevy has an almost new Mercedes or Cadillac as their get-away car.

So it is in the highly imaginative language picturing the groom's approach to the wedding event. It portrays his transportation as nothing less than Solomon's royal couch (or sedan chair), surrounded by an armed guard so large that it stirs up a dust cloud resembling "columns of smoke." Nothing is too good for this wedding—gold, silver, and expensive spices all have their part.

I don't know if we should equate the armed guard with the groomsmen. But if so, we might compare the daughters of Zion with the bridesmaids. At any rate, the daughters of Zion have had a part in preparing for the event (3:10).

> "A *wasf* is an Arabic love song in which the lover praises the physical attributes of his or her partner" (Hess, p. 31).

They are also commanded to gaze upon the crowned groom on this his special day (verse 11). Wedding crowns for both the bride and the groom were a part of Jewish wedding ceremonies up until the destruction of the Jerusalem Temple by Rome in A.D. 70 (Pope, p. 448). It was the couple's royal day.

In Song of Solomon 4:1-7 the scene shifts from the arrival of the groom to his description of the bride. Up to this point in the Song it is the young woman who has had the most to say. But that changes in chapter 4, with the groom at last finding his verbal legs. In verses 1-7 and 9-15 he sets forth his admiration of his beloved in two extravagant songs or *wasfs*.

"How beautiful you are, my darling" is the key phrase in his first song. He begins and ends the *wasf* with similar words (verses 1, 7). The sentences in between explain *how* she is beautiful. Beginning with her captivating, peaceful, dovelike eyes he moves to her flowing hair which cascades over her shoulders, reminding him of a flock of sheep descending a hill. Now that particular description probably wouldn't "turn on" most young men today. But if you were a shepherd it might be just the thing.

He is especially appreciative of the whiteness of her teeth, reminding him of a flock of ewes, each with twins (verse 2). While that might not be so extra special to us moderns, we need to remember that a full set of good white teeth before the days of modern oral hygiene made such a "flock" much more rare and special. Her smile obviously attracts him. Next he alludes to the rest of her facial features, which are partially hidden, and apparently provocatively so, behind her veil (verse 3). Men are visual in their sexual appreciation. It has apparently always been that way. Even though males may like what they see in a woman they still enjoy imagining what there might yet be to reveal.

Moving down from her face, the groom describes her as having a strong neck, "like the tower of David," with the appropriate ornaments (verse 4). Once again, a muscular neck may not be a prime attraction for those in a "refined" culture, but for those in societies in which everyone had to work strenuously to keep the family from the ever-present fear of starvation, physical strength in a woman was not only something to be admired but a necessity.

And being a male, of course, he does not overlook her breasts. But here the texture of his remarks shifts radically from the military simile of the tower of David to the much softer (and caressable) image of twin fawns, "which feed among the lilies. Until the cool of the day when the shadows flee away" (verses 5 and 6). He likes that symbolism. Apparently he has not forgotten that back in Song of Solomon 2:16, 17 she had invited him to "pasture his flock among the lilies. Until the cool of the day when the shadows flee away."

While he might be the type of young man who may have a hard time remembering to take out the garbage, he still never forgets some things. And fawns and feeding among the lilies are two of them. I don't know if he is permanently distracted or not, but he stops his description with her breasts and tells us he is ready to go to the (her?) mountain and hill of good smells and pleasures (verse 6). I will let you figure out what he may be insinuating. Meanwhile, he closes his first *wasf* by declaring again that he finds "no blemish" in her (verse 7), using the same word as Leviticus of an offering good enough to present to God (Lev. 22:20, 21).

"The purpose of this *song of description* (vv. 1-7)," David Hubbard writes, "is not evaluation. . . . Its purpose is a public celebration of her worth to him and his consequent commitment to her. By carefully detailing that worth in images compellingly attractive to the ancient, Middle

Eastern eye, he is underscoring how much he loves her, how deeply he wants her, how firmly he intends to stay with her. What she may have looked like to others is irrelevant. Her beauty is in the eye and heart of the one who beholds her. By the song of description he singles her out, praises her to the sky, and pledges himself to her till death do them part. It is not to compare her to other women but to exclude all other women that he sings this song" (Hubbard, p. 305).

Not a bad idea! This is a tune that every young groom (and a lot of old jaded ones also) needs to learn to sing.

6. Marital Pleasures
(Poem III, Part B)

Song of Solomon 4:8–5:1

[8]*"Come with me from Lebanon,*
>*my bride,*
May you come with me from
>*Lebanon.*
Journey down from the summit
>*of Amana,*
From the summit of Senir and
>*Hermon,*
From the dens of lions,
From the mountains of leopards.

[9]*"You have made my heart beat*
>*faster, my sister, my bride;*
You have made my heart beat
>*faster with a single glance of*
>*your eyes.*
With a single strand of your
>*necklace.*
[10]*"How beautiful is your love, my*
>*sister, my bride!*
How much better is your love
>*than wine,*
And the fragrance of your oils
Than all kinds of spices!
[11]*"Your lips, my bride, drip honey;*
Honey and milk are under your

> *tongue,*
> *And the fragrance of your garments*
>   *is like the fragrance of Lebanon.*
> [12] *"A garden locked is my sister, my*
>   *bride,*
> *A garden locked, a spring*
>   *sealed up.*
> [13] *"Your shoots are an orchard of*
>   *pomegranates*
> *With choice fruits, henna with*
>   *nard plants,*
> [14] *Nard and saffron, calamus and*
>   *cinnamon,*
> *With all the trees of frankincense,*
> *Myrrh and aloes, along with all*
>   *the finest spices.*
> [15] *"You are a garden spring,*
> *A well of fresh water,*
> *And streams flowing from*
>   *Lebanon."*

> [16] *"Awake, O north wind,*
> *And come, wind of the south;*
> *Make my garden breathe out*
>   *fragrance,*
> *Let its spices be wafted abroad.*
> *May my beloved come into his*
>   *garden*
> *And eat its choice fruits!"*

> **5** *"I have come into my garden,*
>   *my sister, my bride;*
> *I have gathered my myrrh along*
>   *with my balsam.*
> *I have eaten my honeycomb and*
>   *my honey;*
> *I have drunk my wine and my*
>   *milk."*

> *"Eat, friends;*
> *Drink and imbibe deeply, O*
>   *lovers."*

The first half of Poem III (3:6-4:7) left the young suitor almost breathless with anticipation. He has described his woman friend as only one truly in love could do. Now he stands on the brink of something momentous.

Ellen Davis suggests that "there are good reasons to think that this section [verses 8-15] has been carefully composed to serve as the center of gravity for the whole book. The most obvious indication of the importance of this section is that here, for the first time, the man addresses the woman as 'my bride.'" And the word doesn't just appear once, but some six times in the second half of Poem III (verses 4:8, 9, 10, 11, 12; 5:1). "Accordingly, many regard this as a marriage scene" (Davis, p. 266).

"My bride!" Words loaded with meaning. So is the invitation that accompanies them. "Come with me." He repeats them twice in verse 8. "Come with me . . . my bride." The import of the invitation is clear enough in the context of Poem III. The Poem follows a definite path toward marital union.

1. The groom arrives in royal dignity (3:6-10).
2. He praises her beauty in passionate tones (4:1-7).
3. He invites her to join him as his bride (4:8).
4. He sings a song of admiration, praising her virginity (4:9-15).
5. She has obviously accepted his invitation to come be his bride, because in verse 16 she invites him to come "into his garden" and "eat its choice fruits!"
6. He accepts her invitation to full sexual intimacy (5:1).

From that outline it is clear that Song of Solomon 4:8 is the pivotal verse. He is inviting her to be his bride, to link her life with his that they might in the words of Genesis 2:24 be "joined" together as "one flesh."

The invitation "to" is clearer than the invitation "from" in verse 8. That is, the flow of the poem spells out their new life together, but the full implications of the reference to Lebanon, Amana, Senir, Hermon, lions, and leopards remain open to speculation. One possible interpretation is that she herself must choose to depart her place of protection, that she alone can accept his invitation to go with him. As Richard Hess puts it, "her lover thus calls her to leave her 'fortress' and to open to him the joys of her companionship and love. As he does this, he addresses her as 'bride' and thereby lays claim to her presence with him." (Hess, p. 141).

The song of admiration beginning in verse 9 appears to be a reinforcement of the invitation. "Come with me" (verse 8) because "you have made my heart beat faster" (verse 9). His invitation is not couched in the cold, calculating language of a good business deal in which families merge their assets, but in the passionate phraseology of the truly smitten. As we might say of his condition today, he is turned on and can't get turned off. His heart beats out of control and he is intoxicated (her love is better than wine) with the sight and smell of her (verse 10). But his song does not ignore the power of the sense of touch. In verse 11 he speaks of her lips being as honey. And the mention of the treasures "under" her tongue "points to the depth and fullness of the kissing" (Hubbard, p. 308).

> "Akkadian proverbs describe a woman as a garden of delight" (Walton, p. 579).

But passionate kissing is one thing and sexual intimacy another. That truth emerges graphically in verse 12 in which he twice refers to her as a "locked garden" and once as "a spring sealed up." In ancient Near Eastern literature and in Proverbs 5:15-20 fountains and gardens are erotic symbols. Proverbs 5, for example, counsels a young man to drink from his wife's "cistern" or "well" that his "fountain" might "be blessed" and that her "breasts" might "satisfy" him so that he would be "exhilarated always with her love" rather than with the affections of an "adulteress."

With those connotations and the further context of Poem III in mind, we see the groom affirming that his bride "is not a garden or fountain open to every passer-by; she is rather a *locked* garden, a *sealed* fountain" (Longman, p. 155). In spite of their deep, passionate kissing (4:11) and her fantasies and desires (1:4; 2:4-6; 3:1-5), she has even been a "garden locked" and a "spring sealed up" to him. But that will soon change (4:12).

Meanwhile, Song of Solomon 4:13-15 describes her garden. As with her imagery of the coming of the groom in Solomon's sedan chair in Song 3:7-10, his depiction of her garden is exotic in the extreme. The most expensive herbs and perfumes are the stuff of her garden:

- Myrrh, one of the ingredients in the anointing oil for priests (Ex. 30:23-25) and one of the gifts of the wise men to the Christ child (Matt. 2:11), had to be imported from Arabia, Abyssinia, or India.
- Nard or spikenard, the "very costly perfume" that Mary used to anoint Jesus' feet (Mark 14:3), was "made from the flowers of a

plant growing on the slopes of the Himalayas (thirteen thousand feet in elevation)" (Walton, p. 579; Freedman, vol. 2, p. 813).

- Saffron was expensive because it took the crushed residue of some 4,000 flowers to produce an ounce (Walton, p. 579).
- And so on for the rest of the spices mentioned. All of them were expensive and most of them imported. They were not for the poor but for royalty and the very rich.

In short, the groom's description of the bride and her garden was as equally royal as her portrayal of him arriving as King Solomon. They appreciate each other as lovers should. And, we might note, most lovers do have a high estimation of each other *before* marriage. The secret of a good (rather than a mediocre or poor) one is to maintain that attitude *after* marriage. Of course, if appreciation of one's spouse remains hidden in the heart it won't do much good. It needs to be expressed on a regular basis. We must learn a lesson from the Song's bride and groom—that we need to learn songs of appreciation for each other and express them on a regular basis as we journey through life together.

The groom sums up his appreciation of his bride in Song of Solomon 4:15. She is nothing less than a valuable "garden spring, a well of fresh water," and like the cool fresh "streams flowing from Lebanon." That description, of course, is fraught with double meanings. Such fluids not only nourish the land, but they are also just what this lovesick young man desires.

And that desire will not have to wait long now. The young woman, his bride, in verse 16 signifies her acceptance of his proposal in verse 8 to come with him. But she goes further than mere acceptance. She offers him an invitation that he cannot fail to understand. His bride invites him to "come into his garden and eat its choice fruits." Her invitation is explicit. The Bible uses "coming into" or "going into" as shorthand for sexual intercourse (see, e.g., Gen. 16:2).

This young man who has been dreaming of feeding "among the lilies" (4:5) doesn't need a second invitation. The time is right. He is her king, and she is his queen; he is her groom, and she is his bride. They come together in full intimacy.

The story picks up again in Song of Solomon 5:1, in which the new husband says, "I have come *into* my garden." Note he is speaking of a past event. He has enjoyed her spices and tasted her honeycomb and drunk of her wine and milk. And he enjoyed every bit of it.

The good news is that God made human sexuality to be enjoyed. One of the ongoing joys of biblical life for husbands and wives is the pleasure of each others' gardens. From the perspective of the Song it might be said that God wills for each of us to be exuberant and persistent gardeners who not only enjoy working the soil but also find pleasure in its fruits.

Meanwhile, Poem III closes with the chorus (probably the daughters of Jerusalem, but perhaps also God and the angels) urging the young couple (and us) on in their mutual enjoyment:

> "Eat, friends;
> Drink and imbibe deeply, O
> lovers" (5:1).

That's good advice for every married couple.

Part IV

Aftermath

Song of Solomon 5:2–8:14

7. Frustration and Delight
(Poem IV)

Song of Solomon 5:2-6:3

> [2]*"I was asleep but my heart was*
> *awake.*
> *A voice! My beloved was knocking:*
> *'Open to me, my sister, my darling.*
> *My dove, my perfect one!*
> *For my head is drenched with dew,*
> *My locks with the damp of the*
> *night.'*
> [3]*"I have taken off my dress,*
> *How can I put it on again?*
> *I have washed my feet,*
> *How can I dirty them again?*
> [4]*"My beloved extended his hand*
> *through the opening,*
> *And my feelings were aroused*
> *for him.*
> [5]*"I arose to open to my beloved;*
> *And my hands dripped with*
> *myrrh,*
> *And my fingers with liquid*
> *myrrh,*
> *On the handles of the bolt.*
> [6]*"I opened to my beloved,*
> *But my beloved had turned away*
> *and had gone!*
> *My heart went out to him as he*

spoke.
I searched for him but I did not
 find him;
I called him but he did not
 answer me.
[7]*"The watchmen who make the*
 rounds in the city found me,
They struck me and wounded me;
The guardsmen of the walls took
 away my shawl from me.

[8]*"I adjure you, O daughters of*
 Jerusalem,
If you find my beloved,
As to what you will tell him:
For I am lovesick."

[9]*"What kind of beloved is your*
 beloved,
O most beautiful among women?
What kind of beloved is your
 beloved,
That thus you adjure us?"

[10]*"My beloved is dazzling and*
 ruddy,
Outstanding among ten thousand.
[11]*"His head is like gold, pure gold;*
His locks are like clusters of dates
And black as a raven.
[12]*"His eyes are like doves*
Beside streams of water,
Bathed in milk,
And reposed in their setting.
[13]*"His cheeks are like a bed of balsam,*
Banks of sweet-scented herbs;
His lips are lilies
Dripping with liquid myrrh.
[14]*"His hands are rods of gold*
Set with Beryl;
His abdomen is carved ivory
Inlaid with sapphires.

¹⁵*"His legs are pillars of alabaster*
Set on pedestals of pure gold;
His appearance is like Lebanon
Choice as the cedars.
¹⁶*"His mouth is full of sweetness.*
And he is wholly desirable.
This is my beloved and this is
my friend,
O daughters of Jerusalem."

6 *"Where has your beloved gone,*
O most beautiful among women?
Where has your beloved turned,
That we may seek him with you?"

²*"My beloved has gone down to*
his garden,
To beds of balsam,
To pasture his flock in the
gardens
And gather lilies.
³*"I am my beloved's and my*
beloved is mine.
He who pastures his flock among the lilies."

Weddings are wonderful!
The pleasures of the wedding night are exquisite!
Honeymoons are a joy!

But they come to an end. Then begins the weeks and years of "real life" as the couple live together. That wouldn't be so challenging if people were perfect. But we're not. And living with another person brings forth issues that starry-eyed lovers haven't foreseen. C. S. Lewis put it nicely when he wrote on the dynamics of his own marriage: "A sinful woman married to a sinful man; two of God's patients, not yet cured" (Lewis, p. 49). Not a bad description of the kind of people who after marriage expect to spend their lives together.

Problems do arise. One of those is rhythm. That is the one on center stage in Poem IV.

We might view Poem IV as a short dream-sequence play with six acts.

Act 1 (5:2-7) opens with the bride claiming that she was sleeping but her heart was awake. Now with a statement like that we might expect that what follows might not always meet the strictest standards of logic. We've been warned. Our bride is probably in that never-never land of being half asleep, half awake. She is in bed alone and hears her husband knocking (verse 2).

He is apparently desirous and "ready for action." But she isn't. The time is not right to her. She puts him off with a couple of good excuses (verse 3).

But his insistence and her dreaming that he put "his hand through the opening" (again remember that the symbols in the song often have double meanings) arouses her (verse 4). In her excited state she envisions herself jumping out of bed and rushing to the door to let him in (verses 5, 6).

But he had gone, having better things to do than fruitlessly wait for her. His time of desire has passed. But hers has just arrived. In desperation she searches and calls for him, but to no avail (verse 6).

Her dream soon transforms from one of longing into a full blown nightmare as she rushes out into the city, only to be abused by the city guards who disrobe her, apparently mistaking her for a prostitute (verse 7).

The dream has gotten as bad as it can get as it shifts to Act 2. Here she enlists the daughters of Jerusalem to help her in her desperate search. If they find her husband they are to tell him that she is sick with love (and desire) for him (verse 8).

At verse 9 the dream jumps to Act 3, in which the daughters of Jerusalem teasingly ask our young bride what kind of a husband she has if he could desert such a most beautiful woman.

Their question sets her up for a full blown description of her loved one in Act 4 (verses 10-16). Tom Gledhill points out that "the girls would not be able to recognize the lover from this description; it would not help them to recognize him in the crowd. It is rather an expression of how the girl feels about him. If it borders on the realm of fantasy, . . . that is the way of love." He goes on to note that perceived and actual reality can be very different. In this particular portrayal "we must make some attempt to get into the emotional frame of mind of the poet and his girl. Like any work of art, the poem seeks to create an illusion, an atmosphere" (Gledhill, p. 183).

Her description of this most "outstanding among ten thousand" man (verse 10) is no less moderate than his was of her. It falls into two parts.

The first deals with his head (verses 11-13). An old saying depicts the ideal man as being "tall, dark, and handsome." I don't know if our groom was tall, but she certainly extols him as dark and handsome. Rhapsodizing about his bronzed skin, wavy black hair, enchanting eyes, and delightful cheeks, she saw him as more than extra special.

The second part of her *wasf* moves to the man's torso, which she pictures in terms of a statue. Dianne Bergant (p. 71) helps us see that "the metaphors used follow the same pattern" for each body part.

"(v. 14a) his arms [hands]   rolls of   gold
 (v. 14b)   set with   jewels
 (v. 14c) his belly [abdomen] block of   ivory
 (v. 14d)   covered with   sapphires
 (v. 15a) his legs   columns of   alabaster
 (v. 15b)   set upon   bases of gold"

Our bride closes her description with a return to his head, noting that "his mouth is full of sweetness" (verse 16), a phrase that might refer either to his kisses, the kind and loving words he utters, or, most probably, both.

She addresses her final words to the daughters of Jerusalem, who had in verse 9 teasingly questioned what was so special about this man that she would risk her reputation (verse 7) in seeking him. She has the last word, telling her friends that "he is wholly desirable" and that he was not only her beloved but her friend (verse 16).

Her description has something special about it. As Dennis Kinlaw notes, "our hero is her lover, but he is more: he is her friend" (Kinlaw, p. 1234). Happy is the marriage that has friendship at its center rather than mere physical sexuality. That friendship, of course, is closely related to having a mouth "full of sweetness." Kind words and considerate actions are the necessary foundations for sweet kissing in the long run.

Our bride's dream shifts to Act 5 in Song of Solomon 6:1. The daughters of Jerusalem, apparently convinced of her beloved's value, ask how they can help her find him.

But, as fuzzy as dreams are, she informs them in Act 6 (verses 2, 3) that she doesn't need their help in locating him. Everything has worked out satisfactorily. They have finally gotten the timing of their desires coordinated.

The groom is enjoying her "garden" and gathering "lilies." He is experiencing all her femininity. And she is exhilarating in his masculinity. In the dream's final verse she echoes their mutual pledge of faithfulness and exclusivity that she proclaimed in Song of Solomon 2:16: "I am my beloved's and my beloved is mine" (6:3).

I like Poem IV. It echoes reality. Even good marriages have their ups and downs. The down in this poem centered on a very human problem. Somewhere C. S. Lewis describes it well. For most of his life he had been a bachelor. But marrying finally at age 56, he discovered problems that he hadn't imagined in his celibate days. To his amazement and frustration, sometimes when he was sexually worked up his wife didn't seem to have the slightest interest. But other times when she was ready for action he couldn't see what all the bother was about.

Things haven't changed all that much in 3,000 years. It was the "timing" problem that set off the dream sequence of Poem IV. But as its conclusion demonstrates (6:2, 3), lovers can eventually get their act together. A good marriage has its rough spots, but one of the lessons of Poem IV is that if we continue to be positive and persistent, things can and will work out.

Good news for our bride and groom!

Good news for us also!

8. Loving Affirmation
(Poem V, Part A)

Song of Solomon 6:4-7:5

4"*You are as beautiful as Tirzah,*
    my darling,
  As lovely as Jerusalem,
  As awesome as an army with banners.
5"*Turn your eyes away from me,*
  For they have confused me;
  Your hair is like a flock of goats
  That have descended from Gilead.
6"*Your teeth are like a flock of*
    ewes
  Which have come from their
    washing,
  All of which bear twins,
  And not one among them has
    lost her young.
7"*Your temples are like a slice of a*
    pomegranate
  Behind your veil.
8"*There are sixty queens and eight*
    concubines,
  And maidens without number;
9*But my dove, my perfect one, is*
    unique:
  She is her mother's only
    daughter;
  She is the pure child of the one

who bore her.
The maidens saw her and called
her blessed,
The queens and the concubines
also, and they praised her,
saying,
¹⁰'Who is this that grows like the
dawn,
As beautiful as the full moon,
As pure as the sun,
As awesome as an army with
banners?'

¹¹"I went down to the orchard of nut
trees
To see the blossoms of the valley,
To see whether the vine had
budded
Or the pomegranates had
bloomed.
¹²"Before I was aware, my soul
set me
Over the chariots of my noble
people."

¹³"Come back, come back, O
Shulammite,
Come back, come back, that we
may gaze at you!"
"Why should you gaze at the
Shulammite,
As at the dance of the two companies?

7 "How beautiful are your feet in
sandals,
O prince's daughter!
The curves of your hips are like
jewels,
The work of the hands of an
artist.
²"Your navel is like a round goblet
Which never lacks mixed wine;

> *Your belly is like a heap of wheat*
> *Fenced about with lilies.*
> *³"Your two breasts are like two fawns,*
> *Twins of a gazelle.*
> *⁴"Your neck is like a tower of*
> *   ivory,*
> *Your eyes like the pools in*
> *   Heshbon*
> *By the gate of Bath-rabbim;*
> *Your nose is like the tower of*
> *   Lebanon,*
> *Which faces toward Damascus.*
> *⁵"Your head crowns you like Carmel,*
> *And the flowing locks of your*
> *   head are like purple threads;*
> *The king is captivated by your*
> *   tresses."*

Appreciation of one's spouse is a wonderful thing. But it doesn't do much for the marriage unless it gets verbalized.

That is exactly what the new husband does in Song of Solomon 6:4-10. It is not the first time in the book. Song of Solomon 4:1-7 had a very similar appreciation sequence, also advancing from her eyes to her hair to her teeth. And in both sequences the key word is "beautiful." In fact it brackets both passages at beginning and end (4:1, 7; 6:4, 10). In his eyes she is the most beautiful person he has ever met. Nothing and no one outdoes her in that category. She has totally swept him off of his feet.

Whereas the praise poems of chapters 4 and 6 share many common elements, they also have some distinctive differences. The first of them shows up in verse 4, in which he compares his beloved to Tirzah and Jerusalem. Jerusalem everyone recognizes as the capital city of Israel and the site of the Temple. But what about Tirzah? The book of Joshua tells us that it was a city captured in the Israelite invasion of Palestine (Joshua 12:24). It later became the capital of the Northern Kingdom of Israel after the nation divided in the time of Solomon's son, Rehoboam (1 Kings 4:17; 16:8, 9, 15, 17), a status it enjoyed until Omri transferred the capital to Samaria (16:24). Archeological excavations of Tirzah suggest a city of natural beauty and well-built houses. It was a city "renowned for its beauty and strength" (Hess, p. 200).

Most modern women might not find it particularly flattering to be compared to cities. But that might not seem so strange in the ancient world. The Bible often likened cities to women. Perhaps Jerusalem and Babylon are the two most well-known comparisons (see Isa. 47 and 54). The compliment implied by the male would not be lost on his lover. To him she was as beautiful as the two most delightful cities he could imagine.

She was not only beautiful, but "as awesome as an army with banners" (6:4). That phrase is a second point of difference from the poem in 4:1-7. It appears again in verse 10, thus forming a bracket around the praise poem of verses 4-10. The word "army," not being in the Hebrew, has been supplied. But it is a good one in the context. The phrase may not imply that she is terrifying. It might hint that she is "splendid to look upon" (Gledhill, p. 192). But there was power there. Roland Ehlke suggests that "this is hardly a gentle description of the woman! . . . It emphasizes the hold she had on him. She came, she saw, she conquered. Especially does she conquer him with her eyes" (Ehlke, p. 197).

> "'Terrible as an army with banners': if this army were approaching you, you would indeed be afraid. It seems that he finds her so disturbing that he has to beg her to turn her eyes away" (Knight, p. 32).

That thought brings us to the third innovation in chapter 6's appreciation poem. Her eyes are not merely beautiful as in 4:1. Here in 6:5 they are threatening, so much so that he asks her to turn away from him. She has such power that "she can unnerve him with a single glance" (Garrett, *Proverbs*, p. 417). One gaze, we might say, "turns him on."

The fourth innovation in chapter 6 occurs in verse 8, in which the groom compares the women in the large royal harem to the beauty of his bride. The numbers are not as important as their ascending order. The king may have 60 beautiful queens (those of highest rank in the harem), 80 concubines (a group of women who had sexual functions in the court), and unlimited maidens (those not yet officially in the harem, but women that the king could choose from if he so desired in the future), but "however many royal beauties, consorts, maidens there may be, our girl outshines them all in the radiance of her dazzling splendour" (Gledhill, p. 193).

None can compare with her. She is his "unique" and "perfect one." And everyone knows and admits it (S. of Sol. 6:9).

Verse 10 contains the final innovation from the appreciation poem of chapter 4. Who is this? is the cry of our young groom.

- Her presence brings brightness like the rising sun.
- Her complexion is as fair as the moon.
- Her personality is as pure and radiant as the sun.
- She is spectacular in every way—"as awesome as an army with banners."

The praise song began in verse 4 with the male comparing his bride to the best of cities. It ends in verse 10 equating her with celestial bodies. And in between (especially in verses 8 and 9) he noted that she is beyond comparison, that she is the best of all women.

In the appreciation poem of verses 4-10 we find one of the most important ingredients of a successful marriage. What is it, I need to ask myself, that I notice and comment on about my spouse? Is it her imperfections and problems? Or do I go out of my way to mention the best points? Let's face it, flawless people simply do not exist. It is my daily choice as to whether I pick at my spouse's "warts" or uplift the beauties and qualities that attracted me in the first place. To follow the latter course not only betters our marriage in ways we can't even imagine, but it is to imitate God who loves us in spite of our imperfections. It is that kind of godlike appreciation that finds an outlet in words and actions that makes our beloved feel appreciated and eventually flows back in kind in the sort of relationship that God meant marriage to be.

With verses 11 and 12 we come to one of the most obscure passages (especially verse 12) in the Song of Solomon. It is even difficult to determine whether the male or the female is speaking.

Richard Hess, in reflecting on verse 11, suggests that "the stroll around the garden is a stroll around the body of the lover. It is a description of the beauty of the lover's body as well as suggesting the pleasures of love that await the speaker" (Hess, p. 207).

As to verse 12, George A. F. Knight suggests that its "exact meaning is now beyond recovery" (Knight, p. 34). Tremper Longman hazards that "the most definite point we can make about this verse is that it expresses strong passion, most likely of the woman for the man. Her passion has so overwhelmed her that she is 'caught up' and discovers herself transported into the man's chariot," which might be the "traveling coach" or "sedan chair" of Song of Solomon 3:7, 9 (Longman, p. 187).

Song of Solomon 6:13 finds the chorus (perhaps the daughters of Jerusalem) calling for the bride to return that they might gaze upon her. The verse sets the stage for the groom to gaze upon and describe the female in the appreciation poem of 7:1-5.

Verse 13 is the only place in the Song to refer to the woman by a proper noun. "The name 'Shulammite,'" Knight suggests, "derives from the Hebrew root *sh-l-m,* from which we get the noun *shalom,* meaning 'peace.' Solomon's name also comes from this root." Thus Shulammite might simply be the "feminine form of Solomon, one that becomes Salome in Greek" (Knight, p. 35). If the latter interpretation is correct, then the name is a part of the royal symbolism that runs throughout the Song.

Song of Solomon 7:1-5 again has the male admiring his bride. If Song of Solomon 6:13 set him up for gazing, it is gazing he does. And he likes what he sees. Beginning with her sandaled feet, his eyes run up her legs to her hips (7:1); navel and belly (verse 2); breasts (verse 3); neck, eyes, and nose (verse 4); and hair (verse 5). We should note that the only clothing mentioned are the sandals of verse 1. After that it is the male gazing and perhaps gasping at the glories of her very feminine body. It appears that the author has here captured the mood of the Bible's first marriage scene: "the man and his wife were both naked and were not ashamed" (Gen. 2:25). Excited undoubtedly but not ashamed. The Song of Solomon is a correction to those types of religious prudishness that find problems with what God declared to be "very good" at the end of the sixth day of creation (Gen. 1:26, 27, 31). He created men and women to enjoy each other within the secure bounds of committed married love.

By the end of Song of Solomon 7:5 the groom discovers himself captivated, as he put it, by her tresses. The seductiveness of hair has been around for a long time. We find examples of the power of hair to snare a man in ancient Egyptian love poetry.

> "With her hair she lassos me,
>   with her eye she pulls (me) in,
>   with her thighs she binds,
>   with her seal she sets the brand."

Again,

> "[Her ha]ir is the bait
> in the trap to ensnare [me]" (Hess, p. 218).

The tantalizing tresses of Song of Solomon 7:5 may only have been one part in the groom's entrapment, but trapped he is. In verses 6–9 he will express his yearnings for intimacy.

9. Inflamed Desire
(Poem V, Part B)

Song of Solomon 7:6-8:4

[6]*"How beautiful and how delightful*
you are,
My love, with all your charms!
[7]*"Your stature is like a palm tree*
And your breasts are like its
clusters.
[8]*"I said, 'I will climb the palm tree,*
I will take hold of its fruit stalks.'
Oh, may your breasts be like
clusters of the vine,
And the fragrance of your breath
like apples,
[9]*And your mouth like the best*
wine!"
"It goes down smoothly for my
beloved,
Flowing gently through the lips of
those who fall asleep.

[10]*"I am my beloved's*
And his desire is for me.
[11]*"Come, my beloved, let us go out*
into the country,
Let us spend the night in the
villages.
[12]*"Let us rise early and go to the*

vineyards;
Let us see whether the vine has
    budded
And its blossoms have opened,
And whether the pomegranates
    have bloomed.
There I will give you my love.
[13] "The mandrakes have given forth
    fragrance;
And over our doors are all choice
    fruits,
Both new and old,
Which I have saved up for you,
    my beloved.
8 "Oh that you were like a brother to me
    Who nursed at my mother's
    breasts.
If I found you outdoors, I would
    kiss you;
No one would despise me, either.
[2] "I would lead you and bring you
Into the house of my mother, who
    used to instruct me;
I would give you spiced wine to
    drink from the juice of my
    pomegranates.
[3] "Let his left hand be under my
    head
And his right hand embrace me."

[4] "I want you to swear, O daughters
    of Jerusalem,
Do not arouse or awaken
    my love
Until she pleases."

To put it mildly, our young groom had become quite worked up by the time he had completed his poem of admiration in Song of Solomon 7:1-5. Beginning in verse 6 he starts to graphically portray his desire for intimacy. He finds her totally "delightful," a word used only here in the Song, but one that sums up his feelings for her.

Back in verse 5 he told us that her "tresses" had captivated him. But his fascination with her far transcended her hair. In verse 7 he compares her figure to a stately palm tree and pictures her delectable breasts as clusters of sweet dates.

But by verse 8 he is ready for more than mere looking or contemplation. He tells her that he desires to "climb the palm tree" and "take hold of its fruit." The author leaves nothing to the imagination here. He is ready for intimacy in every way. Richard Hess notes that verse 8 "evokes an erotic scene of lovemaking symbolized by the male fantasizing his ascent on the date palm and his taking hold of the clusters of fruit" (Hess, p. 221). His fascination with her breastly fruit continues on into the middle phrase of verse 8 when his mind transmutes them from date clusters to grape clusters. From that point he moves on to his desire to kiss her in the latter part of verse 8 and all of verse 9.

My guess is that many Bible readers skip over such passages as the groom's very graphic expressions of desire. For them such "nastiness" has no place in the Bible. Sex is something you do in the dark when God "isn't watching." Such a mindset, as we noted in the introduction to the Song, led the medieval commentators to conclude that they couldn't really be reading what the words were saying. Thus they allegorized the book to represent Christ's love for the church.

But it is just because of such wrongheaded, perverted thinking that God put the Song in the heart of Scripture. From a biblical perspective married sexuality has nothing wrong with it. There may be perverted people, but it is the Creator God who made maleness and femaleness and commanded them to become one flesh (Gen. 2:24). The God who created taste buds and delightful flavors to titillate and satisfy them also endowed male and female sexual organs with all their sensuous feelings and explosive potential. In short, it was God, as my seminary teacher Charles Wittschiebe put it, who "invented sex."

It is the devil who has perverted it in two major ways. First, to lead people to make it cheap, casual, and dirty. Second, to lead "good Christians" to believe that it is nasty and not to be enjoyed, even inside the bounds of marriage. OK, some of them might suggest, you might have to "do it" or "endure it" for the sake of having children, but only a person weak in spirituality and love for God could actually "enjoy" it. *Not so!*

blares out the Song of Solomon. God made humans male and female in all their sexual complexity to enjoy how He fashioned them. The Song is a call for married Christians to abandon prudishness and begin to experience the joy of the physical beings that God made them to be.

If the explicit sexual yearning turns off certain "pious" individuals, it certainly doesn't offend the Song's young bride. In Song of Solomon 7:10 "the female interrupts the musings of the male because she can no longer contain her desire. She picks up the poetry and imagery of her lover to co-incide her own senses of love and desire with his" (Hess, p. 223).

> "I am my beloved's,
> And his desire is for me."

Her's is the cry of full commitment that is the necessary foundation for intimacy. Their desire and commitment is mutual, as we see from the parallel passages in Song of Solomon 2:16 and 6:3.

But verse 10 has even more than mutual commitment. The wording of the text brings to mind Genesis 3:16: "To the woman He said, . . . 'your desire will be for your husband, and he will rule over you.'" Here in Song of Solomon 7:10, John Snaith asserts, "we seem to have an echo of Gen. 3:16 in reverse: whereas there the woman's husband is to rule over her, here the man's passion for the woman is such that she controls him—a radically different situation!" (Snaith, p. 110). But it seems to me that Snaith takes the reversal too far and in the process misuses an important point. Othmar Keel's understanding reflects a more biblically accurate position: "In the same way that her yearning and passion were directed toward him, his passion and yearning are now directed toward her. Thus the curselike situation is lifted, and the brotherly/sisterly equality given in creation is restored. Love is experienced as a return to paradise" (Keel, p. 252).

Song of Solomon 7:10-8:3 represents the bride's invitation to intimacy. She has not only recognized the strength of his desire for her (verse 10), but she herself has become excited at his graphic sexuality. Thus in verse 11 she, perhaps in her imagination, invites her lover to accompany her to the rural countryside where they can spend the night together. The symbolism in verse 12 of vineyards, grapes, and blooming pomegranates has the sexual overtones that we find throughout the Song. Her body is a fruitful place (see verses 7 and 8), and he has previously enjoyed her "garden" to the full (5:1). But if for some reason he has trouble understanding the symbols, she tells him plainly that "I will give you my love." They can enjoy together all the "choice fruits" that she has "saved up for" her "beloved" (7:13).

Her imagination soars aloft in Song of Solomon 8:1, in which she wishes he were like a brother who she could show physical expression to in public without being condemned by the community. G. Lloyd Carr points out that "she is not wishing that they were literally brother and sister, but that they had the freedom of public expression of their love. What was not in good taste even for husband and wife was perfectly permissible between brother and sister" (Carr, p. 166). Her wish at this point was "*not sexual* but is a desire to be free to show her love for the groom freely and openly" (Garrett, *Proverbs,* p. 424), since "apparently any public show of affection . . . , even [between] a husband and wife, was severely censured in Israelite society at this time" (Garrett, *Song,* p. 247).

But public expression wasn't all that she desired. She also pictured in her imaginings taking him to her mother's house where she could give him "the juice" of her "pomegranates" and he could put his left hand under her head as he caressed her with his right (8:2, 3).

The bride closes off her musings by again addressing the daughters of Jerusalem, warning them not to squander their affections and hearts (verse 4).

10. Affirmation and Commitment
(Poem VI)

Song of Solomon 8:5-14

> [5]"Who is this coming up from the
>   wilderness
> Leaning on her beloved?"
>
> "Beneath the apple tree I
>   awakened you;
> There your mother was in labor
>   with you,
> There she was in labor and gave
>   you birth.
> [6]"Put me like a seal over your
>   heart,
> Like a seal on your arm.
> For love is as strong as death,
> Jealousy is as severe as Sheol;
> Its flashes are flashes of fire,
> The very flame of the Lord.
> [7]"Many waters cannot quench love,
> Nor will rivers overflow it;
> If a man were to give all the
>   riches of his house for love,
> It would be utterly despised."
>
> [8]"We have a little sister,
> And she has no breasts;
> What shall we do for our sister

On the day when she is spoken
for?
⁹"If she is a wall,
We will build on her a battlement
of silver;
But if she is a door,
We will barricade her with
planks of cedar."

¹⁰"I was a wall, and my breasts
were like towers;
Then I became in his eyes as one
who finds peace.

¹¹"Solomon had a vineyard at
Baalhamon;
He entrusted the vineyard to
caretakers.
Each one was to bring a
thousand shekels of silver
for its fruit.
¹²"My very own vineyard is at
my disposal;
The thousand shekels are for you,
Solomon,
And two hundred are for those
who take care of its fruit."

¹³"O you who sit in the gardens,
My companions are listening for
your voice—
Let me hear it!"

¹⁴"Hurry, my beloved,
And be like a gazelle or a young
stag
On the mountains of spices."

The marriage has taken place. The honeymoon is over. The community, including the daughters of Jerusalem, have enjoyed the celebration and appreciated the couple's affection for each other.

It is the community chorus that we hear in verse 5a: "Who is this coming up from the wilderness leaning on her beloved?" Of course they know who it is. But just as the similar question in Song of Solomon 3:6 focused all eyes on the arrival of the groom, so here the question of the chorus centers our attention on the returning couple. The image of "leaning" symbolizes their mutual dependence.

In verses 5b-7 the scene shifts to the bride who had just awakened her husband's love and passion "beneath the apple tree" (verse 5b). She goes on to discuss with him the power of committed love in verses 6 and 7. Tremper Longman makes an important point when he notes that this "is the only place in the Song that really steps back and reflects on the nature of love itself" (Longman, p. 206). Elsewhere it is just assumed.

The description comes in two phases. Verse 6 sets forth the positive aspect of love. It "is as strong as death," the one force powerful enough to affect every living thing and from which they cannot escape. Perhaps there is nothing on earth as powerful as death except love. Love is something that people will not only die for, but also live for. It motivates people to do things they would never do for fame or money.

More than being "as strong as death," it engenders "an assertion of the rightful claims of possession" (Carr, p. 170) that verse 6 translates as jealousy. The passage is not employing jealousy in a negative sense here. Rather, its usage is parallel to the jealousy of God, who loves His people so much that he will not let them go without a struggle. He is a "jealous God" (Ex. 20:4) who cares for His people and becomes angry with those who come between His beloved and Himself (see Zech. 1:14-17; Nahum 1:2). Longman observes that "there are only two relationships described in the Bible where jealousy is a potentially appropriate reaction: the divine-human relationship and the marriage relationship. These are the only two relationships that are considered exclusive. Humans can have only one God. If they worship another, it triggers God's jealousy. God's jealousy is an energy that tries to rescue the relationship. Similarly, a man and a woman can have only one spouse. If there is a threat to that relationship, then jealousy is a proper emotion" (Longman, pp. 211, 212).

Longman is quite correct in viewing the language of Song of Solomon 8:6, 7 as pointing toward monogamy. And when anything challenges that very special relationship, love expresses itself as jealousy, whose "flashes are flashes of fire, a most vehement flame" (verse 6, RSV). You may have noticed that the preceding translation differs from that of the *New American Standard Bible,* which renders the Hebrew as "its flashes are flashes of fire, the very flame of the Lord." The difference rests upon the fact that the Hebrew can be translated either as a superlative, "the fiercest of flames," as in the Revised Standard Version, or as the "flame of Yah" or Yahweh, as in the *New American Standard Bible.* If the latter translation is correct, then the author uses the divine name to heighten the description of the flame and perhaps to point to God, who is the source of human love.

The first part of verse 6 elevates the "two shall be one" monogamous aspect of the passage by having the bride claiming that she wants to be like a seal in her lover's life. A seal in Bible times was a mark of ownership. Here the woman declares that she "wants to be wholly identified with her lover's intentions and commitments. Set as a seal, she becomes a visible sign of who this lover is, and what he stands for" (Davis, p. 296).

> ### The Value of Love
>
> "It is a commodity that cannot be bartered or bought. It is free but not cheap. There is no trade for it. Instead, its value is higher than all earthly possessions. Therefore, when it is found or acquired, it must be valued and preserved beyond anything else" (Hess, p. 242).

The second aspect of committed love appears in verse 7a. Here we find the problematic side of love. Every marriage has its challenges. Some of them come from the outside and some from the inside, but committed love is unquenchable. The floods of life cannot wash it away or destroy its spark.

The second part of verse 7 highlights the value of love. It is worth more than anything else in the world. And those who seek to purchase it for money are in for a grand disillusionment.

Song of Solomon 8:8, 9 finds the bride thinking back about her brothers in their protective function. The ancient world highly prized virginity, and they not only viewed her as immature (having no breasts), but as one who needed their help whether she wanted it or not. They saw their situation as similar to that mentioned in Ecclesiasticus 26:10: "Keep strict watch over a headstrong daughter, or else, when she finds liberty, she will make use of it" (NRSV).

The protective brothers envision two alternatives in Song of Solomon 8:9. If she is a "wall," she is safe and will not open her favors to anyone. In such a case they will reward her with silver (jewelry) and gifts to keep her on the right path. But, on the other hand, she might be a "door," who would open herself to invasion. In that case they would build a barricade of cedar planks around her. At any rate, they would at all costs protect her virginity for "the day when she is spoken for" (verse 8).

Verse 10 finds the bride boasting that she had made it to marriage as a virgin. She was indeed a "wall" and had not succumbed to her natural desires until the time was right. But to correct her brothers who saw her as immature (no breasts), she informs them to wake up to the fact that her breasts are now like "towers." She is ready for life with her husband, and her guardians can quit their worrying. She was a woman in whom her husband could rest in "peace" since she had preserved

> ### Thoughts on Being a "Wall"
>
> "The closer we come to the event of marriage the more our hearts taste it in advance. The ultimate intimacy, the complete embrace, is all the more wonderful when we have contemplated its coming and are able to celebrate it in the fullness of covenant commitment and the freedom from fear and guilt that marriage bestows. Pity the persons, and their number today seems legion, who are robbed of the exquisite joy of anticipation by engaging in physical acts of intercourse with persons whom they barely know. Our fast-food style of life may sustain us physically. Its sexual counterpart diminishes our true humanity virtually beyond recognition" (Hubbard, pp. 296, 297).

herself for him alone before marriage and would continue to do so now. All of her words in Poem VI point to her total commitment to her relationship with her man.

Song of Solomon 8:11, 12 contrasts the massive properties of Solomon with the value of the bride's own person. Alluding back to verse 7b, she declares that neither her love nor her person can be bought or sold. The

Solomons and lesser mortals of the world can keep their money and gifts. Her own "vineyard" was hers to give, and no amount of wealth can swerve her from her loyalty to her husband. Their love is priceless.

Such is the commitment that forms the necessary foundation for every successful marriage. Men and women may be tempted toward unfaithfulness by other people or to put their professions or hobbies ahead of their beloved. But such is the kiss of death to extended marital happiness. More than anything else, those who desire a successful marriage need to get their values straight and live them out in daily life.

With verse 13 the Song has come full circle from its opening verses. In 1:2-4 the young woman calls for their separation to end and their intimacy to begin. Here at the end of the Song the male does the same: "Let me hear" your voice. But he is not the only one who is listening. So is the community (the "companions"). We find an important lesson here. A committed relationship is not merely between two individuals "out behind the barn." To the contrary, a healthy relationship and/or marriage is something in which the community rejoices in, even though it has significant times of privacy.

The Song closes in verse 14 with the bride desiring one of those special times of solitude with her groom. She is impatient for him to return and to behave like a "gazelle or a young stag on the mountains of spices" (cf. 1:2-4; 2:17; 4:6). The Song leaves us with her words of erotic desire ringing in our ears. But the longing is not hers alone. According to Song of Solomon 8:13, 14 it is mutual.

The Song has a surprise conclusion. It "does not end with the lovers sitting together in the garden." Rather, "they are still in motion, still straining with desire, still hoping for something that is not given. . . . The Song ends on a note of separation, uncertainty, anticipation of their next meeting." As such, "it is a realistic picture of young love" (Davis, p. 302).

But it is also a faithful picture of our relationship with the God who made us male and female. Life is an existential journey. We live on earth, not in heaven. As a result, our relationship with God parallels that which we have with other humans. Never fully satisfied, we are ever stretching beyond for fuller relationships. The Song's final invitation leaves us with a feeling of desire for our earthly beloved, and, by extension, a longing for our heavenly Beloved who made us in such a way that we can enjoy love here on earth as both a taste of Eden and a foreshadowing of things to come.